Mobile Marketing

Mobile Marketing
Achieving Competitive Advantage through Wireless Technology

Alex Michael and Ben Salter

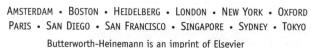

AMSTERDAM · BOSTON · HEIDELBERG · LONDON · NEW YORK · OXFORD
PARIS · SAN DIEGO · SAN FRANCISCO · SINGAPORE · SYDNEY · TOKYO

Butterworth-Heinemann is an imprint of Elsevier

ELSEVIER

Butterworth-Heinemann is an imprint of Elsevier
Linacre House, Jordan Hill, Oxford OX2 8DP, UK
30 Corporate Drive, Suite 400, Burlington, MA 01803, USA

First edition 2006

British Library Cataloguing in Publication Data
A catalogue record for this book is available from the British Library

Library of Congress Cataloging-in-Publication Data
A catalog record for this book is available from the Library of Congress

ISBN–13: 978-0-7506-6747-0
ISBN–10: 0-7506-6747-8

For information on all Butterworth-Heinemann publications
visit our web site at books.elsevier.com

Printed and bound in the United Kingdom

06 07 08 09 10   10 9 8 7 6 5 4 3 2 1

Contents

Contents

Preface

Since 1995 mobile phones have gone from being high-end gadgets only the wealthy could afford to an essential accessory, now owned by a large portion of the population of the world. Mobile phone technology has also advanced, taking something that used to be the size and weight of a brick and turning it into a slick, fashionable tool. Gone are the days when all you used a phone for was to talk to someone; now the possibilities seem limitless, and mobile technology is promising new applications and services that will change the way people live and work. The integration of the Internet, mobility and communications at the device, service and transport levels creates a new set of business opportunities. The business challenge is to bring together the three worlds with services that customers will pay for.

The impact of this convergence is not very clear. The structure of the new mobile data landscape is far more complex than the traditional voice-oriented business models and SMS. There is so much hype about how mobile will do this or that, and how mobility changes traditional business models, but there is limited understanding of exactly what this means for companies and their bottom line.

Attention has turned to revenue and revenue sharing – and with good reason. Mobile operators are looking for revenue models, which are able to both ensure a return on the large investments, and make it attractive for content providers to develop and market mobile services.

Through our firsthand experience of the mobile space over the past 10 years we will give practical advice on how you can position your company in the mobile market, and in such a way as to take advantage of new technologies as they emerge. We look at the impact mobile marketing has had on the overall marketing mix and how to understand the needs of mobile users for you to implement your mobile strategy and develop it into the future. We take a detailed look at local markets around the world and view how each local market is developing. With detailed case studies of our own work, we provide examples of where our methods have been successful. The mobile phone is now an essential part of any business strategy, and could be the key to the future growth of your company.

Welcome to the World of Mobile Marketing!

Alex Michael and Ben Salter

Acknowledgements

Alex Michael:

I'd like to thank Chris Hoar for his interesting visions on the mobile world, I'd also like to thank Michael Ohojuru for being such an inspiration over the years.

Ben Salter:

I'd like to thank the team at Sprite for all the support whilst writing this book and my friends and family for giving me sweet words of encouragement to help me on the way.

Chapter 1

The wireless revolution

In the last five years we have seen the IT sector move its focus away from personal computing to mobile/wireless communications. Mobile phones have been gaining in popularity, and encroaching into the realms of PDAs and laptop computers. However, it's not just the popularity of mobile phones that has been so interesting to the marketer, but also the explosion of multimedia services. We have entered a new era – the 'all mobile', era in which mobile phones do it all. Many who will read this book will have seen it in the Internet explosion, and if you are lucky enough to be as old as me then you will have seen it in the desktop publishing era. Marketing has changed. Let's look back a few years and try to define the foundations of the mobile era.

Mobile phones have become much more than entertainment handsets. Consumers already expect a high-end electronics experience from their state-of-the-art digital cameras, camcorders and game consoles. They are beginning to expect that same experience on their mobile phones, with a broad range of compelling, interactive content. Current 3G handsets now feature high-resolution colour displays, integrated video cameras, audio and video content streaming, Internet access at broadband speeds, location-based services, and multi-user 3D gaming. These rich computing environments will encourage and facilitate the development of business applications for mobile phones. We are finally seeing the convergence of the PDA, the mobile computer and a telephone in a single device.

High-speed data transmission with UMTS/3G is widely available in most countries around the world. This has made mobile services more user-friendly, and mobile browsing more practical. The sheer power to transmit more information in a shorter timeframe means that connecting to any remote device is practical.

Mobile browsing is showing the strongest potential for growth in mobile services, as voice has become a commodity and SMS traffic levels are reaching an upper limit. Thirteen per cent of mobile subscribers reported accessing news and information via a mobile browser in June 2004. A marked gender difference characterized mobile browsing, with 17 per cent of men subscribers and 9 per cent of women subscribers using their mobile phones to access news and other information. Browsing activity was driven by a need for context-sensitive information. Over half of all browsers sought weather information (57 per cent), and more than 40 per cent of browsers accessed maps and directions (41 per cent), sports scores and sports news (44 per cent), national news (44 per cent), and movie and entertainment listings (40 per cent). When it comes to news and information on your mobile phone, subscriber propensity to consume has to do with who foots the bill, according to m:metrics. Mobile browsing is ushering in an era of 'always on, always with you'.

SMS is no longer the only way to bill mobile services. The arrival in the mobile world of other, more traditional, billing methods is shaking up revenue-sharing. To make it as easy and quick as possible to pay for content, Bango.com, one of our WAP partners, determines the best payment option and presents this first. This decision is based on your country, your network operator and the amount of money you want to spend.

The mobile phone provides people with a novel way of satisfying their need to communicate, to stand out from their peers and to stay informed. It is important to remember from the outset that the mobile phone did not create this need; rather, it has always been here.

Mobiles really took off in 1996, becoming fashion accessories for all. Although pre-pay vouchers were still around the corner, the cost of monthly subscriptions was finally within most people's grasp. The phones were bulky, there was no SMS, and reception was poor. For schoolchildren (who wouldn't be able to afford a mobile phone for another year or so), a new range of flashy transparent pagers was all the rage. The growth in the number of mobile phones in use has brought with it some significant changes, not only on a technological level but also in terms of the impact on society. The involvement of the mobile phone in the basics of everyday life has been a much more gradual process.

Anyone who is interested in how mobile phone use has developed and grown will look to the Japanese model, which provides a useful case study. Not only has NTT DoCoMo had inconceivable commercial success in Japan with its i-mode brand, but the mobile phone has also reached the point where it is now a presence across all sections of Japanese society.

The Japanese model

In Japan, the mobile phone has been integrated into social and cultural life. Three reasons are given for this phenomenal growth in mobile phone usage in Japan: the mobile phone is personal, portable and pedestrian.

The mobile phone is personal

When your mobile phone is switched on, your cellular network provider knows exactly where you are in the world to within 100 metres or so. At any one time, your phone is usually able to communicate with more than one of the aerial arrays provided by your phone network. They're 10 or 20 kilometres apart (less in cities), and it's usually within range of at least three of them. Therefore, by comparing the signal strengths and time lags for the signals at each station, your network can triangulate your position and work out where you are. This is true whenever your phone is switched on, whether you're using it or not, because every so often it sends out a check signal to make sure everything is working as it should be.

The mobile as a personal statement

Your phone reveals a great deal about who you are. This desire for individuality can also be seen in the straps and accessories which people in Japan use to decorate their handsets, and the clip-on fascias that are used to customize the external appearance of handsets all over the world.

Users want to customize their handset as a way of injecting their personality into a characterless piece of technology. Whole businesses have grown around this personalization, and have been a key driver of mobile web access, both in Japan and elsewhere, with ringtone and wallpaper downloads proving to be the most popular sites on the mobile web (see Figures 1.1 and 1.2). Our own experience of building an MMS distribution system to send out wallpapers with fashion statements has helped the UK market to perceive the mobile phone as a fashion accessory.

The Japanese term for the mobile phone – *keitai* – means 'something you carry with you'. People's mobile phones say a lot about their online social lives that they can carry with them wherever they go. The mobile has become a proxy for the information and social connections that are always at hand. People want to be connected and online any time, anywhere – and mobile phones provide this.

The mobile phone is portable

The mobile industry is no longer just the delivery of voice on a cellular phone. The introduction of data services, multimedia content and advertising

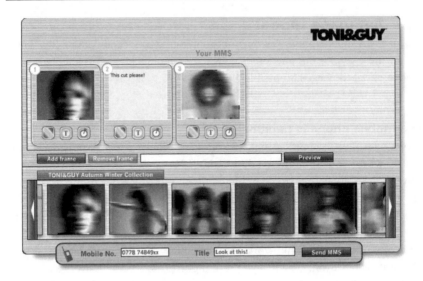

Figure 1.1 *TONI&GUY hair fashion for both MMS messaging and wallpaper distribution*

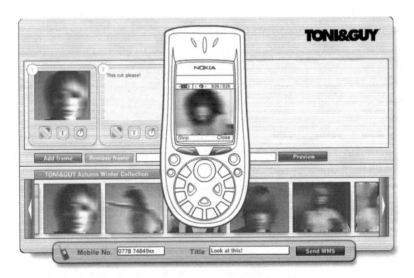

Figure 1.2 *Once you compose your MMS, you can then test it on your selected device before sending it out*

means that many different types of companies are becoming involved with mobile phones. Media companies such as Reuters and Bloomberg now offer their business information through mobile phones. Entertainment companies like Disney sell cartoon characters and advertise via mobiles. It would be more accurate to think of the mobile phone as a device that provides what has been called 'always on, always with you' connectivity, of which voice is just one component. Among young people in Japan, for instance, it has been observed that the mobile phone is not so much a phone as an e-mail machine; for their counterparts in Europe and elsewhere, SMS text messaging plays a similar role. For young people use to surfing and communicating online with e-mail, instant messaging and the web, the mobile phone is the most important everyday tool that they have.

Mobile phones are intimately tied to an individual, to an extent that colleagues and friends would never answer a mobile phone that belongs to someone else – even a spouse. In Japan, even a spouse looking at someone else's handset uninvited is socially unacceptable behaviour. When you call a mobile phone, you have a pretty good idea who will be on the other end of the line. Japanese teenagers much prefer to call their friends on their mobiles, as it allows them to avoid talking to a parent. It also provides young people with a real sense of freedom. In North Africa, pre-paid mobile phones have been credited for providing greater independence for young women.

The mobile phone is pedestrian

The mobile phone is pedestrian, both in that it is used while on the move and in that it has become a mundane, everyday item, according to Mizuko Ito (see below). Mobile phones provide a short-term engagement that has been compared to a coffee or a cigarette break as a kind of 'refreshment'.

It is now illegal to use a hand-held mobile phone when you're driving, even when you're stationary at traffic lights or in a queue of traffic in most countries. Usage includes making or receiving calls or pictures, text messaging, and accessing the Internet. You must always pull over to a safe location prior to using the phone – risk using a hand-held mobile phone when driving, and you risk a fine. You can also be prosecuted for using a hands-free mobile phone if you fail to have proper control of your vehicle.

Inbetween time

You can use a mobile phone to play a game while travelling on the bus to work, to listen to the radio while standing in the queue at the supermarket, or to catch up on the latest news headlines when you've got time on your hands. You have your mobile phone with you all the time, and you can use it to fill the downtime between your other activities.

Cameraphone users still prefer to use a traditional camera or a higher-quality digital camera for what they consider to be their important photos, and cameraphones are used instead to capture what Mizuko Ito refers to as 'fleeting and mundane moments of everyday life'. Ito's own 'Bento Moblog'1, the website to which she uploads daily cameraphone snapshots of her children's lunchboxes, is just one example of this idea being put into practice. Mizuko Ito is a cultural anthropologist who studies new media use, particularly among young people in Japan and the USA. Her research group at Keio University studies mobile phone use and its effect on society.

Specifically universal

Carriers don't have a really strong track record of selling mobile marketing services. They're yet to provide 3G users with a compelling reason to use video calling, and selling MMS as 'like SMS, but a picture' didn't work out too well. MMS is finally starting to see some momentum as a content platform and delivery device, but many carriers still don't have much of an idea on how to sell users on P2P MMS. In Japan, however, there are many specifics of the Japanese context that have led to such widespread acceptance and adoption of mobile phones. Cultural differences between continents or even between neighbouring countries – to say nothing of legal restrictions and other rules and regulations – can lead to variations in mobile usage and habits and the effective provision and marketing of mobile services.

The desire to communicate more easily and have more timely access to information is universal. Many of the observations made by Mizuko Ito and her colleagues regarding mobile phone use in Japan apply equally to mobile markets all over the world.

Mizuko's paper, Technologies of the Childhood Imagination: Yugioh, Media Mixes, and Otaku, *is a transcript of a keynote address she gave at* 'Digital Generations: Children, Young People and New Media', *a conference organized by the Centre for the Study of Children, Youth and Media, at the University of London, 26–29 July 2004.* It is an interesting insight into the future generation and how mobile use is just a transparent part of everyday life.

Location, location, location

Analysts are already predicting that location-based services will play an important part in the development of the mobile Internet. One of the most obvious technologies behind LBS is positioning, with the most widely recognized system being the Global Positioning System (GPS). Location-based services answer three questions:

1 Where am I?
2 What's around me?
3 How do I get to where I want to go?

They determine the location of the user by using one of several technologies for determining position, then use the location and other information to provide personalized applications and services. Traffic advisories, navigation help (including maps and directions) and roadside assistance are natural location-based services. Other services can combine present location with information about personal preferences to help users find food, lodging and entertainment to fit their tastes and pocketbooks. The fact that mobile phones are used on the move means that any information delivered to a phone can be rendered more useful if it is tailored to the user's location. If you search for a pizza restaurant on a mobile Internet search engine, for instance, you want the results to be sorted based on how near they are to wherever you happen to be.

Recent research

The gender gap

A piece of research we recently did for a client in the entertainment industry brought out some interesting results. For us, probably the most interesting revelation was that there is no gender gap when it comes to mobile game play. With the voice service penetration levelling out, mobile service providers are looking for new ways to generate revenue. Mobile content providers utilize successful Internet content in mobile phones to generate revenues. Creative mobile content will help earn big bucks for mobile content providers. There is a rapid expansion in mobile content market, with a sharp increase in 2.5G and 3G handset adoptions. The global mobile entertainment market will reach €18.6 billion in 2006 and will soar to €45 billion by 2009, says a new report from market analysts Juniper Research.

Some of the least-focused mobile content is mobile blogging, mobile books and mobile search. In fact, these particular content areas have tremendous potential to compete with other major content areas by the end of the decade. Mobile books have ability to attract people of all age groups and both sexes. First launched in Japan, mobile books have been a success – full-length novels, short stories and comic books can be read. Cell-phone novels remain a niche market compared with ringtones, music downloads and video games, says Yoshiteru Yamaguchi, Executive Director of NTT DoCoMo.

Regarding mobile games, 31 per cent of female subscribers and 34 per cent of male subscribers report having played in the previous two months. What is interesting here is that men are 65 per cent more likely to download a game than are women. The main reason for this disparity is that too many of the titles available for sale are action/adventure and sports games – genres that are more likely to appeal to men.

Ringtones aren't just for teens

A teenager's penchant for reckless spending, helped along by advertising from ringtone providers has turned the ringtone market over the last five years into a major earner. However, a crackdown of sorts in 2005 began with a code of conduct. In addition, the availability of MP3 from the major record labels is leading to a decline in the traditional ringtone.

North American and European operators are now at work on a code of conduct for ringtone sellers. Operators have been caught off-guard by the activities of several companies selling ringtones. At least one ringtone vendor, Jamster, began selling ringtones in bulk, in exchange for a weekly or monthly fee, in addition to offering a single tone at a time. Some consumers didn't notice the change and thought they were buying a single tone when they were really buying a week's or month's worth. Jamster, however, argues that its pricing is clear. The issue is the subject of a lawsuit, filed recently by Californian parents, against Cingular Wireless, T-Mobile USA and Jamster, which is a subsidiary of the security specialist VeriSign. The suit alleges that the defendants did not clearly state that people were signing up for Jamster's $6-a-month service. By contrast, a single ringtone costs $1.99, according to Jamster's website. Jamster, marketed in Europe under the brand name Jamba, advertises on MTV, Nickelodeon, and websites popular with teens.

Independent ringtone vendors do most of the work of creating the tones: they sign the artists, produce the tones, and distribute them directly to customers. The ringtone vendors also keep a large share of the revenues, with wireless operators keeping a small portion for giving the companies access to their subscribers and for handling the billing. There are growing signs of an operator crackdown, not just with regard to ringtones but also with regard to the games, wallpaper and other add-ons operators sell. We believe that the ringtone segment of the industry will experience a slowdown over the next few years.

In the UK market, the majority of ringtones have been downloaded by subscribers aged 12–25 years; those over 25 years old accounted for 45 per cent of all subscribers who downloaded ringtones. Moreover, more than 65 per cent of those consumers had downloaded more than one ringtone in the previous month. The desire to make a personal statement with a ringtone appeals to a broad range of adult mobile subscribers.

Text messaging has wide appeal

Text messaging can lead to behavioural addictions and increased security risks, according to a renowned psychiatric clinic in Britain which has reported a huge rise in 'technology addictions'. Citing text messaging is an example of such a behavioural addiction, the clinic has noted that some patients spend up to seven hours a day in Internet chat rooms or SMS texting.

Over half – 70 per cent – of subscribers aged 25–34 years had sent or received text messages in the previous month, while 40 per cent of those aged 35–44 communicated via text. Among younger subscribers texting is ubiquitous, with 85 per cent of those age 18–24 sending and receiving text messages. Of those aged over 65 years, 20 per cent use text messaging. Relative to its size, T-Mobile is the market leader in text messaging, with more than half of its subscribers using the service.

Photo messaging is still a fledgling service

More than 60 per cent of subscribers who took a picture with their camera phone had also sent a photo message to another phone or e-mail address in the previous month. 'The fact that people aren't just taking pictures but are starting to send them as well indicates that operator enthusiasm for the service may be well-founded. While the overall penetration of photo messaging is still low, at 7 per cent, Sprint has taken an early lead with 12 per cent of its subscribers sending a photo to another mobile subscriber.

We have been involved in MMS delivery for a number of years, with our most successful campaign for retailing Java applications being the sending of MMS to previous subscribers with sound promoting the game 'Pub Fun Duck Shoot'. From the 10 000 distributed MMSs we had a take-up rate of 5 per cent, which resulted in 500 downloads within the first 24 hours of issuing the MMS. Our experience shows that you can expect response to be near immediate, with traffic still coming in within 24 hours.

Figure 1.3 shows Wanadoo MMS composer, run and developed by Sprite Interactive Limited.

The mobile Internet/WAP

The weather (57 per cent) was the most sought-after information, with more than 41 per cent of browsers accessing maps and directions. Second to this was sports, with sports scores and sports news representing 44 per cent of traffic. National news was accessed by 40 per cent, but the most interesting was movie and entertainment listings of up to 40 per cent. In our view this would be even higher if the information and sites were more available. Table 1.1 shows the European mobile subscriber consumption of content and applications in May 2005.

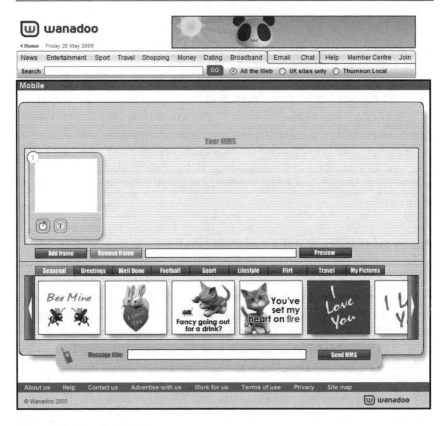

Figure 1.3 *Wanadoo MMS composer*

Table 1.1 *European mobile subscriber consumption of content and applications in May 2005*

Content/application	Percentage of subscribers
Sent or received text	40
Received text message alert	9
Sent photo message	11
Used mobile messenger	9
Used mobile e-mail	18
Downloaded mobile game	5
Downloaded ring tone	16
Downloaded graphic	7
Accessed news via browser	15

When it comes to news and information on your mobile phone, subscriber propensity to consume has to do with who foots the bill. Those with corporate accounts or accounts that are otherwise subsidized by their employer are significantly more likely to use the browser on their handset to access that kind of data, compared with subscribers who are personally responsible for their bill.

Having researched the market, our own analysis shows that consumers want their 3G mobile phones to receive travel alerts, redeem coupons and pay for car parking tickets – to have simple, straightforward functionality both now and in the future. However, voice calls and SMS messaging are clearly currently the main functions of a mobile device. Ironically, media content (such as watching videos or listening to music) was absent from our 'top 10' list. When we asked what the most interesting future function would be, many respondents were looking forward to using their phones to help speed up and simplify various financial transactions.

Today's top 10 mobile functions

1 Voice
2 SMS
3 Alert subscriptions
4 Calculator
5 Taking pictures
6 Mobile gaming
7 Using operator portals
8 Mobile search
9 Surfing WAP sites
10 Alert subscriptions.

Tomorrow's top 10 wish list

1 Travel alerts
2 Parking meter payment
3 Special offers and general marketing communications
4 Season tickets

5 Credit/debit cards
6 Flight check-in
7 Vending machine payment
8 Retail checkout
9 Loyalty cards
10 Mobile coupon redemption.

Chapter 2
Understanding the wireless world

In this chapter we will look at the different types of companies that make up and profit from the wireless world. We'll then take a look at the different technologies and systems in place in the wireless world, in order to give you the basic understanding to make the most of the rest of this book.

There are several types of companies that operate in the wireless world, and the number is growing as the industry expands. All these companies are important parts of the overall structure, and all of them generate revenue from it; they range from the behemoth network operators down to the ring-tone and content aggregators. As the mobile industry has now turned from a specialized technology market to a mass consumer market, practically any company can enter the wireless world; the question that needs to be asked is, how can a company best profit from the range of services on offer?

The main players in the wireless world

1 *Phone users.* These are the end-users who use all the services, whether they are aware of it or not. They are the 'grass roots' of the wireless world.
2 *Network operators.* Network operators are the 'overlords' of the wireless world; without network operators there would be no networks. Each country has a number of competing network operators (see Appendix A). The main network operators in the world are Vodafone, Orange, T-Mobile, O2, 3 Hutchison Telecom and NTT DoCoMo. Operators route messages, bill phone users and collect revenue from them. There is some cross-over with fixed landline operators in some countries, but generally they are separate entities.

3 *Access providers.* These are gateways for companies and mobile networks. They offer companies a window to the wireless network and let them take advantage of the technologies on offer (GPRS, SMS, WAP, etc). An access provider will manage commercial and technological relationships with network operators and will try to guarantee a quality ('always-on') service.

4 *Platform providers.* Platform providers are similar to access providers, except that they go one step further to provide a software-based platform to enable the launch of a mobile-based service. They handle the whole process, from user experience through to network billing and customer support, and because of this they need to work closely with and have an in-depth knowledge of the other service providers in the wireless world.

5 *Content and application developers.* With the advent of rich media browsing on mobile phones, content developers became an essential part of the wireless world – and an important extra revenue stream both for themselves and for the rest of the industry. Sprite Interactive is one of the top content providers in the UK, and this company, like a number of other content providers, will produce topical and entertaining content for mobiles, either to specification or as part of their own in-house catalogue. Examples of mobile content include news streams, ring tones, logos, Java games, videos, Java applications and so on.

6 *Content aggregators and publishers.* These are the companies that sell the content developed by content and application developers directly to the phone users. There can be some cross-over between content aggregators and content developers, but generally the two areas are separate. Content aggregators generally advertise products in magazines and newspapers, from their own web portal and on the television. Examples of large content aggregators are redsuitcase.com (Figure 2.1) and Mob.tv.

7 *Corporate companies.* This group includes all kinds of companies who have an interest in the wireless world as a means of communicating with their customers, employees and suppliers, and generating revenue.

8 *Marketing and media agencies.* These agencies are involved in the wireless world on a strictly consultancy level, advising companies on how best to penetrate the wireless world.

9 *Mobile consultants.* There is usually some cross-over here with access or platform providers. Mobile consultants advise companies on how best to define and implement their wireless strategy.

As briefly mentioned above, there is a large amount of cross-over in the industry between the different types of players. A number of content developers also run sites to sell their content, so can also be defined as content aggregators, and many of the platform and access providers are also aggregators. Each company needs the others in order to best profit from the wireless world. As well as asking

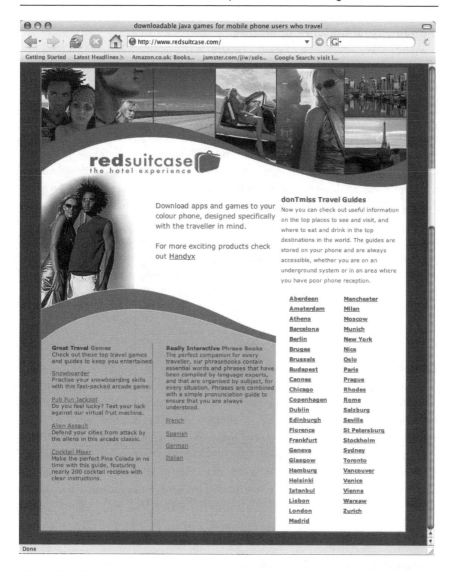

Figure 2.1 *The redsuitcase website, www.redsuitcase.com*

how can they profit from the wireless world, companies also need to ask how much revenue they are going to make once the idea has filtered its way down to and then through all the other companies above them. It is also worth noting that below network operator level there is now a large number of companies offering very similar services, so to get the most from access and platform providers it's best to consider a number of different options. Some of the best and most imaginative mobile content is coming out of smaller, independent development houses.

Mobile virtual network operators

A Mobile Virtual Network Operator (MVNO) is a mobile operator that does not own its own spectrum and usually does not have its own network infrastructure. Instead, MVNOs have business arrangements with traditional mobile operators to buy minutes of use (MOU) for sale to their own customers. Many are familiar with resellers of telecom services such as long distance, local exchange and mobile network services. MVNOs are similar, but they will usually add value – such as brand appeal, distribution channels and other benefits – to the resale of mobile services. An example of a UK-based MVNO that has done this is Virgin Mobile, which provides SMS messaging for as little as 3 p per text. Successful MVNOs are those that have positioned their operations so that customers do not distinguish any significant differences in service or network performance, yet offer some special affinity to their customers. Well-diversified independent MVNOs can offer a product mix that traditional mobile operators cannot match – for example, supermarket MVNOs could offer a package of shopping rewards and benefits. MVNOs have full control over the SIM card, branding, marketing, billing and customer care operations.

Business issues

The major benefit to traditional mobile operators cooperating with MVNOs is to broaden the customer base at a zero cost of acquisition. It is likely that traditional operators will continue to embrace MVNOs as a means of deriving revenue to offset the enormous cost of building new networks. As more MNVOs expand in the marketplace, they are likely first to target prepaid customers as a means of low-cost market entry themselves. MVNOs are a means of encouraging competition, which ultimately leads to greater choice and lower prices.

Wireless technologies

Now we have covered in brief the main players in the wireless world, the majority of the rest of this chapter will be spent looking at the main different technologies in the wireless world. The wireless industry is one based on advanced technology, so before embarking on a wireless campaign or strategy you should arm yourself with the necessary knowledge to be able to understand and take advantage of this technology. The areas that will be covered are WAP and the mobile Internet, messaging (SMS/MMS), i-mode, application environments (Java, Flash, Symbian), and 2G and 3G networks. A number of these areas are covered in much more detail later in the book; this chapter aims to give you the basic understanding of them to begin your journey into the wireless world.

WAP and the mobile Internet

WAP stands for Wireless Application Protocol, and it is the standard by which mobiles and some PDAs access the Internet – so, for example, if you are told to access a WAP site from your mobile, you are accessing a mobile Internet site. WAP is used to deliver information to mobiles and as a gateway to download content, so it is a very important part of the wireless world.

The most recent version of WAP is WAP 2.0, which is a step up from the fairly basic WAP 1.0. It allows the user to download rich content and to have content 'pushed' through to them, and lets developers create pages that are much closer to standard websites in look and feel.

WAP is covered in much more detail in Chapter 13.

Messaging

Without doubt, one of the main areas of growth in the wireless world over the past four or five years has been in messaging. To give you an idea of the vast numbers of messages sent, on New Year's Eve 2004 alone in the UK 111 million SMS messages were sent!

There are four main messaging technologies:

1 SMS
2 Smart messaging (from Nokia)
3 EMS (Enhanced Messaging System)
4 MMS.

SMS was the first of these technologies to emerge, and it started life as a straightforward person-to-person messaging service which succeeded because it was simple to grasp and support for it was so widespread. SMS lets you send and receive messages made up of text and numbers to and from mobile phones (and specially equipped landlines). Nokia created an extension to SMS, called 'smart messaging', that is available on more recent Nokia handsets. This form of messaging can be used for Over The Air (OTA) phone configuration and updates, picture messaging, logos and so on. The value of smart messaging is that messages can be sent over the standard SMS infrastructure and therefore operators do not need to upgrade their infrastructure. EMS emerged between SMS and MMS, and allows the sending of relatively simple media and extended text messages. MMS is a rich version of SMS; it has been accepted as standard by the 3GPP (the mobile standards authority), and it enables the sending of sounds, pictures and video to and between handsets. MMS messages take the form of short presentations, and the use of MMS as a business tool is wide and varied – for example, in animated business cards, greeting cards, cartoons and maps.

SMS

WHAT IS SMS?

The first SMS message was sent in December 1992 from a PC to a mobile phone on the Vodafone network. SMS is currently one of the most widely used wireless technologies, and its usage amongst phone users remains very high. It accounts for around 60–80 per cent of average revenue per user (ARPU) and, though its percentage of total ARPU is decreasing due to the emergence of other communication technologies, its usage will remain steady. In the top 20 European countries over 200 billion SMS messages are sent each month, but the usage of SMS goes far beyond peer-to-peer communication; it is a great business tool for interacting with end-users, and it provides a convenient and widely accepted way of billing the user.

HOW AN SMS MESSAGE IS SENT

SMS messages are generally no more than 140–160 characters in length, and contain no images or graphics. When a message is sent it is received by a Short Message Service Center (SMSC), which must then get it to the appropriate mobile device. To do this, the SMSC sends an SMS request to the home location register (HLR) to find the roaming customer. Once the HLR receives the request, it will respond to the SMSC with the subscriber's status: (1) inactive or active; and (2) where the subscriber is roaming. If the response is 'inactive', then the SMSC will hold onto the message for a period of time. When the subscriber accesses his or her device, the HLR sends an SMS notification to the SMSC, and the SMSC will attempt delivery. The SMSC transfers the message, in a short message delivery point to point format, to the serving system. The system pages the device and, if it responds, the message gets delivered. The SMSC receives verification that the message has been received by the end-user, then categorizes the message as 'sent' and will not attempt to send it again.

An SMS message is made up of two parts. The first is the header, which is the message protocol information, and includes the sender's address, type of coding and message validity. The second consists of the data – that is, the body of the message with the information to be transmitted. An SMS can be interpreted with three types of encoding: 7-bit, which is the code for the Latin alphabet; 8-bit, which is the code for data; and 16-bit, which is used for Greek and Arabic alphabets (the number of characters for 16-bit is limited to 70).

There are two types of SMS transmissions: Mobile Originated (MO) and Mobile Terminated (MT). MO messages are messages sent from a mobile phone; these can be sent to another mobile, a computer or a landline. MT messages are messages sent by the network to a mobile phone. To enable the identification of corporate servers by the networks specific numbers can be used; these are called shortcodes, and are covered in more depth in Chapter 6.

Benefits of SMS as a marketing tool

What would get your attention – a printed letter telling you when the installer is coming to connect your broadband, or a text message the day before, reminding you not to go out? The business use of SMS is wide and varied, and it provides a unique intimate link with your customer base. Sprite Interactive has implemented and carried out a number of SMS campaigns; for an in-depth look at these applications of SMS technology take a look at the case studies in Chapter 14.

Advantages of text messaging as a communication tool include the following:

1 *Texting is reliable.* Text messaging is generally reliable – you're more likely to get a message twice than not receive it at all. Also, as you can tell when a message has been received, you can automatically resend if it hasn't arrived within an acceptable time.
2 *Texting is quick and easy.* Text messages are ideal for getting information to employees who are rarely at their desks, or for sending out information to thousands of customers at the press of a button. Texting has become such a part of everyday life that 'txtspeak' dictionaries have emerged, with characters and words developed specifically to speed up the texting and communication process.
3 *Texting is cheap.* It is generally cheaper to send out text messages than to communicate by phone or direct mail. The pricing model for SMS as a whole is simple; the end-user will pay a fixed rate for each message, and intense competition in the market has helped keep costs low.
4 *Texting is discreet and confidential.* Incoming messages are discreet and will not interrupt the person you are communicating with to the same extent as a phone call. It can be easier to text than to talk, and it does guarantee an extra level of privacy.

MMS

WHAT IS MMS?

The Multimedia Messaging Service (MMS) adds images, text, audio clips and, ultimately, video clips to SMS (Short Message Service/text messaging).

Although SMS and MMS are both messaging technologies there is a dramatic difference between the two of them as far as content goes, with the average size of an MMS message being much larger than that of an SMS message. At the heart of MMS technology is the Synchronizes Multimedia Integration Language (SMIL) application, which allows the creation and transmission of 'presentations' over a mobile phone. These presentations take the form of miniature slide shows, much like a scaled-down version of Powerpoint. SMIL lets the user define what each slide contains, the timing for each slide, and the order in which the slides appear. SMIL data is not necessary and is not supported by certain handsets, but without the SMIL code MMS data is displayed as successive content that the user must scroll through.

MMS messages are sent through WAP – unlike SMS messages, which are sent through GSM. The fact that MMS messages are sent through WAP means that additional network infrastructure has had to be developed. The MMS Centre (MMSC) is the key point of an MMS network. When a message is sent, WAP carries the message between the MMSC and the mobile phone. When an MMS message is composed and sent to another phone, it is transmitted from the sender's handset via WAP to the sender's operator's MMSC. This operator then sends it to the MMSC of the operator of the recipient's handset; the recipient's operator then sends the recipient notification that there is an MMS, and once the recipient opens the notification the MMS is send through to his or her handset from recipient's operator's MMSC. This works in the same way if a subscriber wants to download an animated logo or wallpaper; once the content provider has received the subscriber's request, the provider will send an MMS to the subscriber's operator's MMSC. This operator then sends the subscriber notification, and he or she can then download the MMS in the same way as before. The beauty of MMS is that it provides a complete development and billing environment. Sprite Interactive has worked extensively with MMS since its launch, developing the MMS composer application for Freeserve (Wanadoo). More of Sprite's use of MMS as a business tool can be seen in Chapter 14.

Figure 2.2 shows the Freeserve MMS composer.

MMS is significant because:

1 It is a natural evolution from text messaging, which already has a large user base – especially in Europe and Asia
2 It has support from key operators and industry players
3 MMS messages can be sent to and from e-mail
4 Richer applications can be developed using MMS than with SMS.

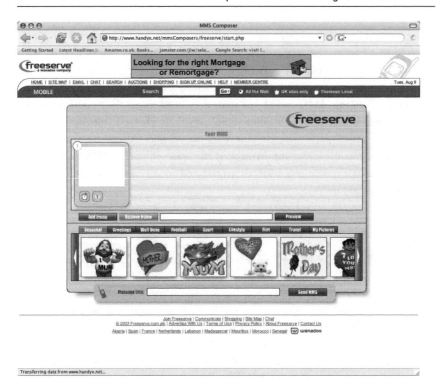

Figure 2.2 *The Freeserve MMS composer*

Unlike SMS communication, MMS communication is not necessarily discreet – i.e. rich media lends itself to being 'flaunted' rather than being discreetly in the background. This trend is already noticeable with richer media such as ring tones. A popular example of MMS in action is photo messaging (using an inbuilt camera to take a photograph and then sending that photograph as a message or an e-mail); other examples of where the technology has been used include:

- weather reports with images
- stock quotations with diagrams
- slideshows of football goals
- animated business cards or maps
- video messages with the use of 3G networks.

MMS has not proved to be as successful as many people in the industry predicted when it was launched, and its use today is mainly for photo messaging. There are several reasons for this. First, there is an education and ease-of-use issue. MMS is not as simple to use as SMS and, as a communications tool, is more on a par with e-mail; it is simply easier to send an e-mail than it is to send an MMS, and it is easier to send an SMS to communicate with someone than it is to send an MMS. With SMS a user can be sent an address to download images or videos onto their mobile; it is easier to follow this kind of message than to receive the same content by MMS, which may also have size restrictions. Moreover, many phones do not come set up for MMS, and phone users may need to call their operator to find out settings, and then have to enter these into their phone manually. This may deter many phone users who do not want to change settings on their phone. Finally, and probably most importantly, is the issue of price. MMS messages are at least twice as expensive as SMS messages, and sometimes more; this is clearly off-putting to phone users.

i-mode

i-mode is NTT DoCoMo's mobile Internet access system, widely popular in Japan. The 'i' in 'i-mode' stands for information. i-mode is also a whole multibillion-dollar ecosystem, and is part of Japan's social and economic infrastructure. Approximately 30 per cent of Japan's population uses i-mode about ten times or more a day, and the system allows them to send e-mail, to book train tickets and to perform other Internet-style activities. There are over 42 million i-mode subscribers in Japan out of a total mobile market of around 70 million, which is a considerable share. i-mode started in Europe (Netherlands, Germany, Belgium, France, Spain, Greece and Italy) in April 2002, and expanded to Taiwan and Australia during 2004.

What is the difference between i-mode and WAP?

Both i-mode and WAP are complex systems. There are several important differences in the way i-mode and WAP-based services are presently implemented, marketed and priced. i-mode uses cHTML, which is a subset of HTML and is relatively easier to learn for website developers than WAP's mark-up language 'wml', many new handsets use html to render web pages. Another difference is that at present in Japan i-mode is 'always on', while WAP systems in Europe operate on a dial-up basis. Another major difference is that at present an i-mode user is charged for the amount of information downloaded plus various premium service charges, while WAP services are charged by connection time.

The success of i-mode

There is no single reason why i-mode has been so successful; its success is due, to a large extent, to the fact that NTT DoCoMo made it easy for developers to develop i-mode websites. In Japan home PCs are not as widespread as in Europe and the USA, so Japanese people tend to use their i-mode handsets more for Internet access than do Europeans or Americans. A low street price to Japanese consumers for i-mode-enabled handsets means that there is a low entrance threshold; this, combined with the general love of gadgets by the Japanese population, has caused the market to become flooded with i-mode-enabled handsets. The i-mode system is also relatively inexpensive to use, being 'always on'; moreover, and the billing system that i-mode uses (micro-billing) makes it easy for subscribers to pay for value-added, premium sites, and is attractive for site owners wanting to sell information to users. The i-mode system has been effectively marketed in Japan as a fashionable accessory, which has definitely helped, and the use of cHTML for site development has led to an explosion of content as ordinary consumers have been able to develop content. The presentation of content has also helped i-mode to grow, as it is so easy to get to grips with, and the AOL-type menu list of partner sites gives users access to a list of selected content on partner sites that are included in the micro-billing system and can sell content and services.

Business applications for i-mode

There are many business applications for i-mode. Both content and services can be sold on i-mode – for example, airlines sell airtickets via i-mode, media companies sell cartoon images via i-mode, securities houses sell shares and investments via i-mode, and Japanese government lottery tickets are sold via i-mode. The subscriber can have a virtually private network on i-mode. Many companies use i-mode for customer relationship management (CRM). Since about one-third of Japan's population uses i-mode practically every day, i-mode allows companies to engage into dialogue or other interactions with a large part of Japan's population.

Application environments

There are currently three main application development environments for mobile phones: J2ME, Symbian and Flash Lite. These three environments are covered in much more detail in Chapter 12, so we'll only look at a very brief overview of the environments here.

J2ME is the environment with by far the most widespread handset support. The majority of games and applications on sale today have been developed in J2ME; it is a versatile environment, and as handsets get more powerful so does Java support. Symbian content is restricted to Symbian handsets – for example, high-specification Nokias, Sony Ericssons (p800/900) and so on. Symbian applications tend to be much richer than J2ME, with enhanced features and graphics, but are generally priced higher. Flash Lite is the newest application environment, but could make the biggest impact of the three once handset support is widespread enough. Flash Lite opens up the Flash environment to mobile developers, which will lead to advanced user interface development, widespread sound and graphic support and universal network connectivity, so developers can create dynamic applications which obtain data from existing web services or download different portions of an application based on what the user is doing on his or her handset.

Mobile generations

What are 1G, 2G, 2.5G, 3G and 4G?

Technically, generations are defined as follows:

- *1G networks* (NMT, C-Nets, AMPS, TACS) are considered to be the first analogue cellular systems, which started in the early 1980s. There were radio telephone systems even before that.
- *2G networks* (GSM, cdmaOne, DAMPS) are the first digital cellular systems, which were launched in the early 1990s.
- *2.5G networks* (GPRS, CDMA2000 1X) are the enhanced versions of 2G networks with data rates of up to about 144 kbps.
- *3G networks* (UMTS FDD and TDD, CDMA2000 1X EVDO, CDMA2000 3X, TD-SCDMA, Arib WCDMA, EDGE, IMT-2000 DECT) are the latest cellular networks, which that have data rates of 384 kbps and more.
- *4G* is mainly a marketing buzzword at the moment. Some basic 4G research is being done, but no frequencies have been allocated. The Fourth Generation could be ready for implementation around 2012.

What is so important about 3G?

The term '3G' refers to the next generation of wireless communications technology, the 'first generation' having been analogue cellular and the 'second generation' (2G and 2.5G) being today's existing GSM/GPRS networks. Today's 3G networks provide high-speed, high-bandwidth support to bandwidth-hungry applications such as full motion videos, video calling and full Internet access. With 3G you can watch music videos, chat with your friends via video calling, send video messages and even watch mobile TV. 3G roll-out has so far been quite slow, but expect to see 3G-enabled applications and content becoming widespread across mobile networks and service providers.

Chapter 3

Marketing for a wireless world

Mobile marketing is the use of the mobile medium as a communications and entertainment channel between a brand and an end-user. This is the only personal channel enabling spontaneous, direct, interactive and/or targeted communications, any time, any place. This channel of marketing is for mobile devices, including handsets, PDAs and laptops. Communications include short message services (SMS), multimedia messaging services (MMS) combining text with simple graphics and sound, wireless application protocol (WAP) mobile Internet and WAP push services, and full multimedia third-generation (3G) services. It is highly personalized, interactive, and has an immediate impact. When used cross-media to complement other promotions, mobile marketing has been proven to generate a solid increase in sales.

The mobile market has a number of clear advantages over traditional media, including the following:

1 Response rates generally are over 10 per cent
2 Recall rates in our campaigns over the last four years have achieved over 70 per cent
3 It is the cheapest form of communication with end-users
4 It has better commission margins than traditional advertising
5 It requires minimal external effort to initiate a pilot.

Revenue-generating services

Today, mobile marketing is not only the telecom specialists' arena; many traditional companies have a real opportunity to do business in this sector. The three main groups of revenue-generating services that can be offered over a mobile phone are:

1 Premium services
2 Online services
3 Offline services.

Premium services

These are services delivered directly to a mobile phone (logos and ring tones, Java games, permission-based content etc.).

Premium SMS is an ideal vehicle to deliver appealing content offerings. It not only enables the instant delivery of exclusive content, services and entertainment, but also converts a phone into a credit card payment system, allowing users to purchase goods by dialling a number or simply pointing their phones at products or vending machines.

Enpocket, based in New York, is developing a premium SMS service that will allow users to purchase event tickets. For a modest service fee and the cost of the ticket, an image with a bar code will be delivered to a user's phone. The bar code can then be scanned to gain entrance to the event.

Premium SMS can also allow payment for very small sums of money – to view online content or to participate in contests, polls or other activities. Because of the associated processing fees, credit cards aren't a viable medium for these tiny transactions. By comparison, adding a modest charge to a user's mobile phone bill is convenient and affordable.

Online services

Online services are those related to mobile phone use and delivered to a support package other than a mobile phone (such as software to be used on the phone), or those unrelated to mobile phone use but delivered via the mobile handset. Figure 3.1 shows the website of www.handyx.net, which uses the web as a presentation tool for all its products. The billing is done through premium SMS. The handyx site illustrates the method of highlighting a short code that drives the billing and, assuming the user has enough credits, the product is then sent 'over the air' (OTA) to the user's phone.

Figure 3.1 *Website www.handyx.net*

Offline services

Many companies from outside the mobile sector have already seen the opportunities in the mobile offline market by retailing goods to mobile services that are not delivered to a mobile phone – for example, theatre tickets. Mobile data services are clearly not their core business, but companies such as media groups and portals now use the mobile phone as a new communications channel, inviting their audiences to vote in television shows, request songs on the radio and download logos and ring tones from their favourite artists, to name just a few of the services on offer.

Services providing goods that are not delivered to a mobile phone include, for example, buying cinema tickets, renting DVDs, paying for parking, settling restaurant bills, or making purchases from a vending machine.

State of the world market

Operators are increasingly looking for applications that entice business users from large companies. Traditionally the business user has been a target segment for operators, and this is now becoming the focus for many operators. This trend is good for application vendors, as carriers look to differentiate themselves through software.

Regardless of the technologies that drive the market, most analysts agree that the wireless market will be sizeable in the next five years. Ovum predicts that the number of users will be 784 million by 2007. A more aggressive figure, provided by IDC, states that by the end of 2006 there will be 1.2 billion wireless users. Some more recent projections predict that this level could be reached in 2005, as sign-up has far exceeded expectations worldwide.

Much of what we have found suggests that North America will probably continue to lag behind Asia and Europe in terms of wireless users. Critics say that the technological limitations of hand-held devices will continue to keep American consumers less interested in these devices for the foreseeable future. The less developed Internet infrastructure in Europe and Asia has contributed to wireless' popularity, whereas high-speed landlines in the United States have set expectations at an unreasonably high level for the hand-held medium. Paralleling the wireless population, worldwide wireless business and consumer e-commerce revenue is forecasted to be concentrated largely in Europe and Asia, but North America will not be too far behind, propelled by the spending habits of the US wireless audience. While now very few devices are able to surf the Internet, the percentage that can do so will increase significantly in the next four years. Of wireless users in the US, most still use their devices for messaging and communications, not for surfing, so perhaps the wireless Internet as a part of daily life is still a way off.

Japan's NTT DoCoMo, with its i-mode system, is a formidable presence in the mobile industry, as it is years ahead of most companies in terms of functionality and sophistication of technology. Already, NTT DoCoMo has invested heavily in AT&T Wireless to introduce its technology to the US. Japanese e-commerce is expected to rise greatly due to the increasing proliferation of wireless devices in the country and, although it will continue to lag behind the US for some time, it is expected to grow considerably in the next five years.

In Europe, Vivendi, a top wireless provider in France, is akin to AOL/Time Warner. It is the world's second largest media conglomerate. In Scandinavia, Nokia and Realnetworks are working together to deliver mobile media players in Nokia's EPOC communicators and phones. These will be able to read RealAudio and RealVideo, and are currently available in all the world markets. Already, Finnish Nokia users can buy Coca-Cola® from machines using an infrared beam on their phones.

It is important to keep in mind that there are very different dynamics working in Europe and Asia compared to the US, and it is very difficult to make direct comparisons. Russia, Japan, China and different European countries all have varying use patterns for phones and even credit cards. For example, in England you pay per minute even for local calls. Credit card use is not common in Scandinavia – at least not as it is in the US. France has long had a system where you can make direct payments by phone. All these factors influence the use and acceptance of wireless, and make it very difficult to provide direct one-to-one comparisons.

While a large portion of the action is happening in Europe and Asia, United States players are becoming more active and hope to expand in the next few years. In the United States, there are three main wireless companies:

1 Sprint PCS
2 AT&T PocketNet
3 Verizon.

Sprint PCS uses CDMA, and has positioned its telephonic side as 'a clear alternative to cellular', while its wireless web features 27 or so companies, including AOL and Yahoo, on its menu. Though relying on CDMA, Sprint PCS and Lucent are testing out the application of 3G technology in the USA, which would allow Sprint to transfer information much faster than it does now.

AT&T, which has seen others pass it by in terms of users, remains in the lead when it comes to revenue per customer. Its target is business consumers, who understandably are valuable customers, though how long AT&T can keep them is debatable, as its outdated TDMA technology frequently prevents some calls from connecting and allows others to be cut off. In order to keep its core and to gain new subscribers, AT&T Wireless is building a next-generation network called 'Edge', which will be compatible with most international networks. CDMA networks such as those of Sprint and Bell Atlantic aren't going to become international, so AT&T has a real advantage with 'Edge' technology as foreign wireless will continue to be more significant in the future. AT&T Wireless is positioned to do well, provided it can switch over without losing too much of its base in the meantime.

The Verizon merger has been a boon to AT&T Wireless. AT&T Wireless has gained a presence in important markets in San Francisco, San Diego and Houston as a result of Verizon being forced to sell licences in multiple markets. AT&T Wireless now has a presence in the top 15 markets in the United States. Verizon offers a wireless service of 32 sites, such as E*Trade, ABC News and Amazon.com, for a modest monthly charge.

While using the same platform to integrate a worldwide network, AT&T and BT (British Telecommunications) Wireless have formed a cell-phone plan called World Connect whereby users can have the same number in 100 countries across Europe, Asia and the Americas. This is the first successful integration of TDMA (US) and GSM (Europe), and might be a sign that single-platform networks may not be necessary. This current deal with BT Wireless may just be a stopgap measure for AT&T until its 'Edge' gets off the ground, but for now it gives them a worldwide presence.

What do we do with our mobile phones?

Mobile phone usage has not really changed much over the last few years, as we still want to keep in touch – by communicating in real time with our friends and family. Other uses have crept into this simple communications tool:

- keeping well-versed – having permanent access to information at any time
- entertainment – taking part in competitions, playing online games or downloading games
- personalization – personalizing our mobiles with ring tones, images or software tools
- work – accessing corporate information and applications directly from our mobile phone.

The mobile market is fast becoming a more open, more universal and more integrated part of the wider multimedia environment. Mobile phones now support more complex applications like those traditionally found only on PCs. Operators are extending their high-speed data networks, making it quick and easy to download and access these applications. The billing model is opening up to include more traditional systems, allowing companies to choose their own billing methods and integrate them more easily in the systems they already have in place. From music and photographic images in the consumer field to CRM or ERP solutions in the corporate world, companies offering all kinds of products and services are starting to take advantage of mobility.

The mobile portal

The mobile portal is where it all happens, acting as a distributor for the content. Mobile content includes entertainment, sports, news, stock quotes, auction bids, ring tones, directions, traffic reports, surveys, games, promotions and advertising. Some examples of 'device-agnostic' content providers include CNN, Disney, InfoSpace, ESPN, CNBC, MTV and EMI (music).

In the case of NTT DoCoMo's i-mode portal, some of the most widely used content – to check concert dates, display Winnie the Pooh as a screen saver, change the ring tone to Beethoven's Fifth – comes courtesy of Cybird. Since its founding in 1998, Cybird has bloomed into Japan's mobile e-commerce colossus. Cybird sells more than 60 mobile services, such as Namidensetsu which, for $2.44 a month, offers information on surfing conditions around the country. Users pay between 80 cents and $2.30 monthly for each service, including ring tones and news updates. The carrier takes a 9 per cent cut, and the licence-holder up to 20 per cent.

A market driven by value-added services

As the market reaches maturity, the business models that underpin the mobile market are also changing:

- voice has become a commodity
- SMS is universal and of low added value, and it is cheap
- voice ARPU (average revenue per user) is falling and SMS ARPU is reaching an upper limit.

Operators are seeking new revenue sources and looking at value-added services (see Figure 3.2), particularly via mobile browsing, to help push ARPU back up.

With voice becoming more and more of a commodity, we are starting to see new types of voice offers – such as all-inclusive offers, where you pay a single fixed monthly fee, no matter how many minutes you call – in some of the more advanced markets. In countries where the penetration rate has not yet reached the

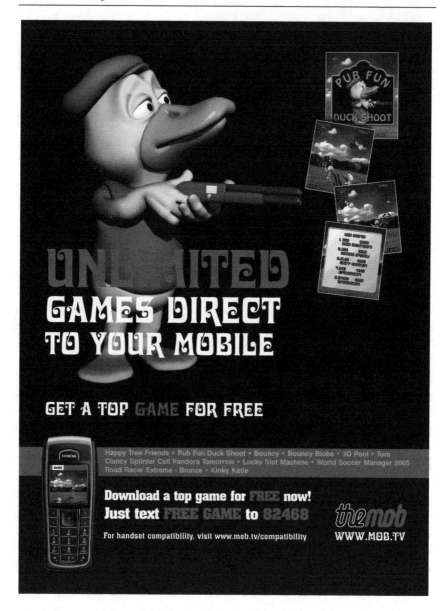

Figure 3.2 *Off-the-page advertising promoting mobile applications*

same level of maturity, there is strong competition between operators to gain new users, who are often prepaid users who spend less than contract users and hence lower the ARPU. This is especially true in China and in Russia. SMS is cheap, universal and of low added value. Strong competition in MO retail pricing has led to a fall in SMS tariffs, particularly in the Netherlands, Germany and, to a certain extent, France. In countries like Spain, where premium SMS has been around for some time now, we can also see SMS use reaching a certain plateau.

A market open to first-time SMS promotions

Following their successful experience with premium SMS, operators want to duplicate the model on other channels to generate additional revenue from mobile data services.

Premium SMS is now available in all countries, with an average range of end-user prices ranging from €0 to €4. Premium MMS is not widely available; currently it is only offered in Belgium, Poland, Switzerland and the Scandinavian countries. All the major operators have launched premium browsing offers, each with specific conditions dictating how other companies can launch their own services. Some of the more successful offers include V-live! (from the Vodafone group), T-Zones (from the T-Mobile group) and i-mode. Although they do not represent a high percentage of the market (less than 10 per cent), the services run through these portals are often quick to turn a profit. It is important to note, however, that this 'open' model only really exists in Europe and, to a lesser extent, in North America. Elsewhere, the dominant position of certain operators, a reluctance to implement this model and the low purchasing power of subscribers have all combined to prevent a third party model that is profitable for all concerned from really taking off.

Increasing marketing efficiency

Today, companies are focusing on wireless solutions that can deliver a faster ROI and increased productivity in their own business. Mobile phones can help to increase productivity in a number of ways, with the growing range of options for mobile voice and data transmission. There are three main areas in which mobile phones can help to increase business efficiency:

1 Customer relationship management – increasing the quality of customer service

- banks can easily and rapidly transmit time-sensitive information
- travel agencies can handle client bookings
- health-care providers can send out appointment reminders to their patients.

2 Corporate usage – improving communication between employees

- transporters can receive and dispatch information on delivery schedules
- sales managers can keep in constant touch with sales teams 24 hours a day.

3 Remote diagnosis from machine to machine

- cars can send a remote diagnosis to the manufacturer's maintenance services units.
- service crews can be alerted automatically when a machine needs repair or stocking up
- advertising billboards can be managed remotely, doing away with the need to send field employees to change the posters manually.

Businesses are witnessing a strategic injection of mobile wireless planning. Where once firms saw wireless initiatives as part of the future with indefinite pay-offs, they now see them as part of the enterprise for operational savings. Today, many view mobile wireless technology as a prime tool for increasing employee productivity and reducing costs for an immediate positive effect on the bottom line.

Analysts agree that despite the economic downshift, mobile wireless technology spending will continue to increase over the next five years. According to a report by Jupiter Media Metrix, IT managers are budgeting for enterprise wireless deployments. In a recent survey of IT executives, Jupiter found that 32 per cent expect to apportion at least $2 million of their budgets to wireless projects within the next three years. However, despite this leaning toward implementing wireless, businesses are cautious and more demanding of return on investment calculations.

Build a better business

Instead of employing mobile wireless technologies to deliver services to customers, many companies are focusing on wireless solutions that can deliver cost reductions through efficiencies and productivity enhancements, which can confer powerful competitive advantages. In particular, many firms are investigating wireless solutions that enable employee collaboration, enhance communication and data access between the field and the office, or streamline key business processes.

In a recent report entitled, 'Ten Key Trends in Mobile eBusiness', IDC Research stated that enterprise applications such as customer relationship management (CRM) and sales-force automation (SFA) will be in the spotlight in the near term, offering firms the chance to derive measurable benefits in both the revenue and cost sides of the equation.

Plan ahead before you start

Mobile wireless initiatives should incorporate components that help increase efficiencies, reduce uncertainties and focus on the bottom line. In a challenging economy, those wireless strategies that will succeed are those that drive savings in the short term, without being short-sighted. With this in mind, the following should be considered when pursuing a mobile wireless strategy.

Think evolutionary, not revolutionary

Firms should see wireless as an extension to their existing wireline data infrastructures. Leveraging a single, open, integratable infrastructure significantly decreases the complexities of implementation and management, and will enable enterprises to scale and evolve to meet future needs. By implementing a wireless solution through existing infrastructures rather than all-new ones, firms will find the results are more manageable networks at lower cost. The focus should be on an open architecture that builds upon and integrates with existing IT infrastructures.

For a strong marketing strategy you need open standards and a scalable platform. Open standards enable firms to select solutions without fear of vendor lock-in in what is a fast-moving industry. This frees firms to choose the best solutions for their individual goals and needs throughout their end-to-end infrastructure-hardware and operating environments. Open standards-based solutions are easily integrated into heterogeneous infrastructures, and allow for optimal cost and performance effectiveness. By utilizing open standards an enterprise can truly 'future proof' its technology investments, and position itself to take maximal advantage of new technologies and business opportunities.

Conversely, best-of-breed solutions designed to meet a firm's individual needs will confer greater return on investment and increased business agility in the short term and beyond. Such solutions bring a community of experienced vendors together to provide customers with a scalable, proven combination of systems, software, financing and support services that provides optimal functionality and performance, minimizes cost and maximizes return on investment.

Wireless is international

The wireless world is an international phenomenon. It is important to remember that while the North American market will amount to something, it will lag behind Asia and Europe in terms of users and e-commerce revenue for some time to come. Scandinavian teens have been using SMS amongst friends to exchange messages on their phones for nearly 10 years, and 82 per cent of people in Finland have a mobile phone while one in four households no longer has a landline.

English has been the dominant language in the world of the Internet – the English-speaking world as a whole accounts for over 80 per cent of top-level Internet hosts and generates close to 80 per cent of Internet traffic. The same may not be true for wireless. The Internet started in the US and the early websites were in English, so those who could easily use the web were from English-speaking countries. For example, Australia has roughly as many Internet users as France despite the fact that France has three times more people than does Australia. It may be assumed that as the Japanese and Europeans have been first out of the gate with wireless, their languages would be dominant. This is not the case; while other languages will have a relatively higher representation in the wireless space than on the Internet initially, English remains the *de facto* world language, especially for business. Any company hoping to do business on an international scale will offer at least an English version to reach a wider audience. Convergence with the Internet is occurring, and eventually all wireless devices may be fully capable of browsing the Internet and providing other functionality, as would a PC, which would only strengthen the spread of English. For at least the time being, a high percentage of wireless and Internet users will be from outside the United States and other English-speaking countries.

Keep your marketing simple

Marketing should strive to achieve three key goals in order for it to be considered successful:

1 It should generate new clients in new markets
2 It should generate more business from existing clients
3 It should improve gross profit margins.

In our marketing armoury we have prospecting, client satisfaction, loyalty programs, competition, competitiveness, market shares and services, and each company is 'commited' to growth by constantly acquiring new clients and optimizing their profitability. A good client is a satisfied client but also a profitable one, with the expected ROI. The marketing message that you deliver will be determined by the goal in mind. For example, the type of communication as well as the message communicated when trying to find and create new clients will be very different from a message sent to existing clients to stimulate additional business. It is vital for the goal of your 'campaign' to be clearly understood before the message and medium are established. With SMS, the situation is no different. Before designing an advertising or marketing campaign using SMS, you need to consider the following:

• Who is the message addressed to – new clients and markets, or existing customers?
• What is the response that you want from customers?
• What is the idea of the message that you want to carry across?

Content is critical

A top-level manager trades a long series of instant messages with another manager. They're debating whether to fire one of their workers.

A woman sends an instant message to her broker, looking to make a quick stock trade and pay her bank account before making an offer on a house.

A doctor shoots off a quick IM to a colleague asking advice about a patient.

Every day, critical information is being shared across the Internet. What has changed in the last few years is that a little less of it is being sent via e-mail. Today, there's a good chance it's travelling via instant messaging initiated by mobile phones.

Regardless of the media, the content that you deliver is vital to your success. It doesn't matter whether you are delivering a full multimedia presentation, a newspaper commercial, an MMS or an SMS – if your message is not clear, your goal will not be achieved. The larger the medium, the more likely your audience may be to see it. However, your aim is not merely for a message to be seen; it must also be understood, remembered and acted upon. SMS places an interesting challenge. With a limitation of only 160 characters, you are forced to think clearly about how you phrase your message. There are also occasionally restrictions on the special characters that some networks and systems support – for example, when sending Unicode characters most providers will limit the characters to 69. As 160 characters is not a lot of space to write a statement that sells, you will need to be economical with the wording that you choose for your messaging. Be sure that the message you write is clear and to the point. If there is a call to action, then this should be kept simple and concise.

Although the number of characters is limited to 160, it is possible to spread a single message across multiple messages – in other words, you could deliver a 320-character message which would simply arrive as two messages. This is done through a process called concatenation. Although concatenation is possible, it is not always recommended. It enables far longer messages, but for the recipient there is the inconvenience of reading two messages. This all means that we can no longer have longwinded product descriptions or large images in our messages; messages need to be more creative and succinct. We need to be more creative in our thinking and descriptions. Thankfully, the culture of personal SMS usage has lent us some help in the form of generally accepted abbreviations (see Appendix A). These help us to create longer messages without the use of the full words.

Best practice for SMS marketing

There are several organizations worldwide that provide guidance on the use of SMS for marketing. Two of these are the Mobile Marketing Association (MMA) and the Institute of Practitioners in Advertising (IPA), both of which are made up of credible people from strong marketing backgrounds. Although both have launched guidelines, the IPA has launched new guidelines for mobile marketing campaigns. The new guidelines have been created by the IPA's Digital Marketing Group, which is dedicated to raising the digital standard of the industry, to help ensure that IPA members utilize best practice, are aware of regulatory requirements and avoid inadvertently 'spamming' when executing their own SMS campaigns or working with mobile marketing agencies and mobile network service providers. The option to 'unsubscribe' from receiving SMS messages is also covered.

The new IPA mobile marketing guidelines have been created to complement existing British Codes of Advertising, Sales Promotion and Direct Marketing, and the ICSTIS Codes of Practice. The IPA recommends familiarization with these codes before embarking on any SMS campaign. The IPA guidelines have been devised by the IPA's Digital Marketing Group, chaired by John Owen of StarCom Motive, with traditional advertising and media agencies in mind, and will prove invaluable when they decide to introduce mobile marketing into the promotional mix. The document is comprehensive and provides guidance on a wide range of topics from consent, response rates, technical and media planning to utilizing third-party SMS databases. This level of detail is not only essential for ensuring that the advertising industry understands the key issues surrounding mobile marketing and how agencies can best exploit this new media to build on brand equity, but also to ensure that SMS remains a viable and effective media option for the long term.

The guidelines recommend that you:

- ensure sender identity is included within the copy of the SMS message and that text language is gauged appropriately to your target audience
- offer the target audience of your SMS campaign the opportunity to 'unsubscribe' from receiving further SMS messages from the outset of the campaign, and further remind them of this in every fifth message thereafter throughout the campaign period
- only send SMS messages to those mobile phones that have specifically 'opted in'
- request that the target audience text a word (i.e. 'YES') as a clear confirmation of 'opt in'
- avoid sending unsolicited SMS messages to your target audience
- provide clear and simple means, in competitions and prize draws, of requesting terms and conditions, and include the identity of the promoter within the SMS competition

- obtain verifiable parental consent before communicating via SMS with minors and seek expert legal advice before commencing such communication.

The Wireless Information Network suggests that opt in for premium rate content services should be gained by a consumer voluntarily sending in a text message (usually an advertised keyword to a shortcode), completing a WAP opt-in page or contacting an Interactive Voice Response line. Free-to-user opt-in can be additionally acquired by using paper-based and web-based registration forms where the user has ticked the box that agrees to third-party marketing.

The guidelines also highlight:

- that SMS media have a successful history of generating high response rates; large volume on-pack promotions have produced response rates ranging from 8 per cent to 20 per cent, and responses from 'opted in' mobile number databases have averaged 15 per cent
- typical mobile marketing reporting metrics and the category of charges associated with SMS campaigns
- technical planning recommendations for high- to low-volume SMS campaigns.

Best practice for third-party SMS database

SMS represents one of the most powerfully intrusive advertising media available in the marketer's armoury. However, this very intrusiveness brings with it a major responsibility for advertisers to use the technique sensitively and ethically. The IPA's Digital Marketing Group new guidelines are the collective work of a team of professionals working together to bring about better clarity to IPA member agencies who are exploring the benefits that mobile marketing has to offer in increasing numbers. These guidelines provide invaluable information for people new to the medium, and a framework to avoid any risk of upsetting the consumer.

Market research and insights

Insights can be obtained by asking people to text in and by sending out specific questions. If an incentive is given to reply, the results are excellent. BBC Radio 1 ran a 'Ten Hour Takeover' on Easter Monday in 2004, which generated 150 000 responses from listeners telling the DJ what music they wanted to hear. The most popular choices were played live on air during the ten-hour period.

Brands aimed at the youth market have had particular success in gaining responses and insights by text – [for example:

> Text us your feedback on Giant Smarties to 0870 123456. You may win £1000

> Have you seen the Heineken promotion yet? Reply yes or no for a chance to win to see Oasis live in Paris

These messages can be sent to a group of people who are briefed to respond, or sent out to people who may have taken part in previous promotions (as long as their permission has been asked).

Voting

People vote by text to express their opinions regarding TV contestants, radio DJ surveys and music playlist choices, and to nominate for music/acting/political awards and contests. However, the technology has a way to go before these lists can be voted on internationally.

When UK operators cooperated to provide person-to-person SMS across networks, traffic grew by a factor of eight times in nine months. In SMS voting, the biggest benefits will be realized when operators cooperate to enable national- and international-scale SMS voting events like TV, radio and other events. The mobile operators have a tried and tested model to follow; they can use the same three principles that make voice mass calling a success.

The first principle is that messages should be terminated in the network that owns the destination number. This host network receives all of the voting messages; the other networks simply route the messages to the host network. This is unlike the SMS voting model currently used in many countries, where individual operators terminate messages to shared shortcodes. Terminating messages in the host network ensures that technical and commercial agreements are simplified and a consistent level of service is provided.

The second principle is that clearly defined interconnect agreements should exist between the operators. As with voice, these agreements define how messages should be routed and when they should be billed. This ensures that subscribers are billed when their votes are counted in the terminating network. This has a subtle and yet vital difference to some current models, where subscribers are billed when their messages are processed in the originating network. In these current models, subscribers can be billed even if their message arrives too late to be counted, and in some cases even if their message is never successfully delivered. For a large competition prize, this clearly is unacceptable. With national-scale SMS voting, subscribers know that 'Message Sent' equals 'Vote Counted'. Votes are counted and are available for display on the television/web as soon as the messages are sent. This positive confirmation and immediacy of participation drives revenues to their peak levels.

The third principle is that accounting rates should be agreed between operators so that the cost of voting and the revenue share between operators is clearly understood. Broadcasters can finally produce the type of programme they want to, with a high-volume vote held in a short period towards the end of the programme. Taking the increased potential of SMS into account, a country the size of the UK might expect to generate almost a billion text messages a year from national SMS voting events – a potential revenue of £300 million to £500 million to share between the operators and broadcasters.

In 2003, WIN facilitated the BBC Sports Personality of the Year text voting service. Previously, WIN had also organized SMS voting for the Brit Awards.

Voting may be part of a marketing campaign, or it can also be used to generate revenue if the user is charged to vote. For example:

Vote for your favourite chart hit and we'll play the top 10 {radio}

Should Ken Clarke win the Tory leadership contest? Vote now. Visit ES online to see how others have voted

Who will win the England vs Albania game?

From wireless vision to market leadership

Because no firm can be certain where its wireless strategy might one day lead, planning for success demands a scalable, extensible data services infrastructure able to integrate new capabilities as business goals and needs evolve. A firm evaluating its wireless opportunities should look for a system's vendor that can leverage strong partnerships with experienced, best-of-breed partners to deliver on a customer's business vision. By selecting a trusted advisor to help guide them from business vision to market leadership, customers can expect to enjoy the benefits of business agility, increased efficiency and effectiveness, and true competitive advantage.

Chapter 4
Improving brand awareness

Interactions through the mobile phone make a deeper connection with a customer, and a more valuable impression. Once you factor in mobile's low cost of creation and high response rates, you realize the true return on your investment compared to other forms of advertising. It has become part of a mobile campaign to look for added benefit from participants sharing messages and forwarding mobile offers to friends. This viral activity lifts participation to further increase the ROI of your program. By building this into your campaign through the design of programs that track and reward participants who forward ads and offers to friends and build buddy lists, you can start with the smallest database that will exponentially grow within weeks.

Brands aimed at the youth market have had particular success in gaining responses and insights by text. BBC Radio 1 ran a 'Ten Hour Takeover' on Easter Monday in 2004, which generated 150 000 responses from listeners telling the DJ what music they wanted to hear. The most popular choices were played live on air during the ten-hour period.

Another example is that of a well-known hairdressing brand that was opening its 287th salon in the UK. The particular problem in this instance was that the business had no track record, but the brand had significant recall. We tried a small test, offering the first 20 people to arrive at the salon on opening day free haircuts, and a further 50 free products. This went out as an SMS to a database of only 500 people, yet on the day we had nearly 300 people turn up, of which a third booked appointments for the future. We did a basic analysis which showed that in total nearly 1500 people responded to the SMS. Of the initial 500, we could only prove that 120 responded.

Making connections

Enhancing traditional advertising campaigns

Companies rely on their brand name to acquire new customers and strengthen their relationship with the ones they already have. Mobile phone technologies can enhance a company's strategies in this area by fostering a personal relationship with the consumer. Mobile interactivity can greatly enhance current advertising programs with direct response capabilities, tracking, and continued customer follow-up. For a small percentage of the overall campaign budget, it is possible to implement a mobile program that can greatly improve the effectiveness of the advertising. It's a great way for a company to show its commitment to its clients, and allows the company to initiate a range of different types of campaigns and promotional vehicles.

The following list is of a few application areas where we have tested mobile programs and they have proved to enhance a more traditional solution:

- direct marketing campaigns
- special offers or product promotions
- chat systems for community building
- branded logos and ring tones
- competitions, quizzes and votes.

Whether the goal is customer retention or acquisition, brand or sales promotion, or the launch of a new project, adding a mobile dimension to a brand-building campaign makes the campaign more interactive, which in turn increases its effectiveness and helps to generate an instant response.

Governmental agencies and NGOs (non-governmental organizations) are dedicated to providing services to their constituents as well as the general public. These organizations have benefited from high-quality mobile services that enhance their commitment to serving people. Making use of a wireless telecommunications service is a way for these organizations to maintain a close relationship with the public, by providing a means to alert, inform, reassure, listen and react promptly in any situation. Examples of its use include:

- real-time alerts, informing the public about emergency situations such as severe weather conditions
- information updates concerning elections, news flashes, cultural events and so on
- voting, surveys and opinion polls that keep in touch with public opinion
- simplification of administrative procedures, such the payment of local taxes.

Building brand awareness

Organizations can integrate wireless communication with traditional and web brand-building activities to extend the impact of the entire branding campaign. Well-developed opt-in promo messages delivered to mobile devices and facilitating people's access to wireless services can move people to your website for interactive branding activities.

Giving customers wireless access to promotions and all the collateral to a conventional website can do a lot to increase brand loyalty. The key questions you need to ask are:

- Are your prospects likely to have mobile devices?
- How can you cost-effectively create a wireless tether to keep customers in the promo or general communication loop?
- Will wireless messages open up new business opportunities?

What about complaints?

Complaint handling is part of brand management – a badly dealt with complaint can damage a brand far more than almost anything else. You must make sure that all complaints are handled as quickly and efficiently as possible, and that your complaint-handling procedures are:

- clear
- transparent
- responsive
- customer friendly.

Direct response communication – the interactive brand

One big advantage of wireless technology is that it enables people to receive information and respond to it immediately from the many places where they may be. Using creative wireless tactics that generate instant response will facilitate the implementation of a consistent strategy.

If you can build wireless links with customers and prospects, instant communication that drives quick action is possible. Wireless devices embedded in products can generate alerts that result in proactive rather than reactive service. First-time buyers can be moved to action faster if they can receive information right when they need or want it. The ability to analyse a targeted prospect's business operations, to determine every action or communication that can be made more effective through speedy wireless data delivery, is vital.

The more people can learn about an organization, the more likely they will be to do business with it. Wireless tactics can educate different groups about a range of topics, such as product or service features, business processes, company rules and procedures, and industry trends. These tactics will improve customer retention, maintain prospects' interest throughout the sales cycle, and help employees to be more effective at their jobs. When an organization's primary purpose is to provide knowledge, wireless technology can magnify the value of this knowledge. Education is answering people's questions, even when they don't know they have questions; it should be easy to determine whether what you sell can facilitate delivering answers to your prospects' various audiences. Customers, journalists, investors and employees are constantly looking for answers. In order to be valuable to the mobile individual, the wireless education your prospects give them has to be 'packaged' in manageable chunks that are easy to navigate, view and sometimes store.

Some products and services are well-suited to being demonstrated through wireless devices, particularly as these devices' computing capabilities increase and new technology such as digital imaging evolves. It is also important to remember that the wireless market consists of not just mobile phone devices but also computers. Individuals equipped with wireless capability for laptops can conduct powerful product demonstrations. If a sales person can use a mobile device during a test drive to show prospects a video clip of how the vehicle performs off-road during the winter, the chance of closing a sale increases. Demonstrating how a new wireless alert feature will improve service delivery will dramatically increase the odds of retaining a customer.

You may need to work with other vendors to deliver some of the components necessary for this type of application; however, if this leads to sales that might not otherwise happen, everybody wins. Digital imaging and the onset of one- and two-megabite mobile phone cameras opens up a whole new way for a brand to interact with its customers.

Enhancing the value of research

Organizations can use wireless technologies, along with the Internet, to enable mobile workers to tap into data that enhance marketing, R&D, consulting services and other operations that rely heavily on knowledge gathering. This technology can also streamline research by making the data collection and reporting tasks automated and near real time. Data collection typically is a tedious, paper-and-pencil driven exercise prone to errors and double data entry. Simply eliminating the need for someone to decipher and process the paper can justify some wireless applications. Once a business learns how to reduce costs while making it easy for anyone to gather data, it should start to find other opportunities to derive benefits.

The Internet has dramatically changed how news is researched and reported. Wireless helps PR agencies to keep pace with these changes by improving their ability to manage PR tasks actually in the field. It also helps to strengthen their relationships with journalists by streamlining and accelerating communication between PR and media contacts.

Wireless is particularly helpful when managing crisis situations. The people with primary roles in this process are often mobile and/or inaccessible when issues arise and they are needed on a client site for direct action. The immediacy of wireless is the best way to keep various audiences – employees, media, customers.

Tactics for successful wireless implementation

Once you have put the campaign together, you need to ensure ongoing customer satisfaction. You need a set of steps in place to help customers to develop, launch and manage an effective pilot test and the deployment of full wireless implementation. How you perceive this process is as crucial as your understanding of the potential of wireless. You can't just drop products on customers' doorsteps and have them fend for themselves. In our experience, you need to call in support – providing tools for calculating ROI and developing the budget, as well as establishing benchmarks and measuring success six months to a year down the line.

Special requirements
Using premium rate numbers
The ICSTIS Code of Practice applies, and you must comply with this in full if you are using premium rate numbers in the UK (see Chapter 8 for further details).

Distance-selling regulations
If you sell goods or services to consumers, then the Distance Selling Regulations for your country will apply to your business. It would be foolhardy not to make sure that you comply with these. They will affect distance selling:

- on the Internet
- on interactive digital television
- by mail order, including catalogue shopping

- by telephone
- by fax
- by advertising on television or radio, in newspapers or magazines.

Marketing particular types of products and services

There are several areas where special requirements are set out in relation to certain types of marketing. What we have provided below is a list of requirements based on campaigns in the last six years.

1 *Adult content.* You must only send marketing relating to adult products or material to recipients who are aged 18 or over, and have specifically consented to receive such adult marketing. Initiatives in most countries for mobile carriers to install age verification procedures and limit unauthorized access to adult entertainment are actually benefiting the demand for content and ensuring a long-term future for the industry as a whole. Mobile network operators can block access to adult-rated material; this move was originally seen by some industry analysts and media commentators as a major setback to the emerging mobile erotica sector, but in reality the number of users of these networks is continuing to grow. The robust age verification platforms are providing the framework for a stable, successful and long-term future for the industry as a whole. It allows consenting adults to access the content they want – a point that has often been overlooked in the past. The mobile industry is creating one of the first properly regulated channels for adult entertainment. The trusted access points are increasing consumer confidence in providing personal information to access adult services. It is clear that since the carrier controls have come in the consumers have become more confident that they are accessing a certified and regulated environment that adheres to all of the appropriate policies and laws. As a result, it is gaining the attention of a new and expanded mobile audience, who feel more comfortable in this environment than on the unregulated Internet. Adult content in a wireless world is discussed further in Chapter 11.

2 *Alcohol.* Mobile marketing relating to alcoholic drinks must not target under-18s (or under-21s in some countries). In some countries it is also illegal to possess alcohol. Sponsorship of text alerts by alcohol brands is allowed provided that the text alert service is not solely or primarily aimed at under-18s, and the sponsorship is done in such a way that it is not intrusive to under-18s who may be signed up to the text alert service.

3 *Betting and gaming.* Mobile marketing in relation to betting and gambling must not encourage addiction to gambling, or be misleading regarding the associated costs or the chances of winning. It must also comply with all relevant regulatory requirements.

4 *Health products and treatments/therapies.* You must be clear about exactly what the product/treatment/therapy being promoted is, or where to find further details about this. Care must be taken regarding mobile marketing in relation to cosmetic surgery. Sponsored text alerts are acceptable, but details of products and treatments/therapies must not be misleading or offensive.

5 *Financial and insurance services.* Mobile marketing in relation to financial services must comply with all relevant regulatory requirements – for example, the FSA requirements or GISC requirements in the UK. The Gramm–Leach–Bliley (GLB) Act requires financial institutions to ensure the security and confidentiality of this type of information. As part of its implementation of the GLB Act, the Federal Trade Commission (FTC) has issued the Safeguards Rule. This rule requires financial institutions under FTC jurisdiction to secure customer records and information.

6 *Weight control.* Mobile marketing in relation to weight control products must not promote being underweight, or be offensive to overweight people. If these alerts are sponsored, you must remember to insert the name of the slimming product or the sponsor.

7 *Motoring.* Mobile marketing in relation to motoring must not encourage drivers to interact with their phone whilst driving or at a petrol station. You must advise users not to use their phone whilst driving.

Location-based mobile marketing

Location-based marketing is based on the location of the recipient at a given time, and the collection and use of location data relating to individuals. This subject has specific legal requirements, in particular those set out in the Electronic Communications Regulations. You must make sure that you comply with these requirements.

In addition:

- you must only send location-based mobile marketing to people who have agreed and opted in to this type of marketing
- the recipient must have a simple, free-of-charge (other than the costs of transmission) means of opting out of receiving any further communications at any time.

When asking people to opt in to receive location-based mobile marketing, you must make it clear that for such marketing it will be necessary to identify the location of their mobile device and therefore their personal location, and also what you will be using these location details for. If you are a network operator or provider, there are some very specific requirements under the Electronic

Communications Regulations in relation to the use of location data and provision of location-based services.

Planning

It is important that the strategic and tactical preparation of campaigns involves a clear, written plan that maps out ROI objectives, business goals, budget, etc. This is the glue that holds everything together, and provides benchmarks that will measure the success of the wireless implementations. It allows you to assess feedback from users and thus ensure that your product or service lives up to the expectations you set during the sales process.

Business strategy

Wireless applications can significantly impact on four strategic marketing operations by reducing costs within each area and/or streamlining processes that increase revenue. You need to work with end-users to analyse the potential impact of wireless in these areas in general, and on your products or services in particular.

The four main areas are:

1　Communicating with existing customers
2　Enhancing customer service and support
3　Communicating with prospective customers
4　Improving internal communication and operations.

Communicating with existing customers

Customers have an established relationship with your brand, so it's easier to measure and reduce the costs of communicating with current customers. You can use wireless activities to mobilize customers into a proactive marketing force, as well as to increase customer retention. This has obvious benefits, but probably the most tangible is that you can measure how it will directly increase bottom-line profits. Figures 4.1 and 4.2 illustrate wireless campaigns for British Gas.

For many organizations, customers are more than the people who buy their products or use their services. They can be journalists, politicians, investors and others with whom organizations do business. Wireless can play a role in increasing the value of these relationships. A very important first question for your prospect is, what is the value of an average customer during the life of that business

Figure 4.1 *Internal wireless campaign for British Gas (Corbis © 2005)*

relationship? Then, how, and by how much, can prospects increase customer retention using your wireless strategy?

Enhancing customer service and support

Hand-held, palm-tops, personal digital assistants (PDAs) and laptops are helping analysts to work more flexibly and efficiently and ensure accurate transfer of results

Figure 4.2 *Brand-building internal wireless campaign for British Gas (Corbis © 2005)*

between in-the-field research and back-end software. Current trends show that hand-held computers and wireless access portals have become increasingly relevant in market research analysis. They seamlessly integrate into corporate information management solutions like quality management systems, and into electronic record management and analytical workflow management tools. Data are entered and automatically sent to a wireless server and from there directly into real-time management information systems.

Providing service and support to both customers and prospects is expensive, and wireless can significantly reduce these costs. Service and support are such key contributors to customer retention and helping organizations to gain a competitive advantage that they deserve their own place as a strategic category. Wireless can increase the response time and efficiency of field service, while transforming service calls into potential sales opportunities. Embedded wireless devices can add new dimensions to customer support that lead to preventative rather than reactive responses to meet customers' needs. If your product shaves ten minutes off of each sales call, what is the total financial impact for your prospect? If you eliminate office-staff data entry of field-service paperwork, can prospects assign those office workers to more productive tasks? What new business opportunities does your technology open up?

Communicating with prospective customers

Given wireless' limitations, don't expect to see many product orders coming through PDAs from first-time buyers. In the home, Wi-Fi has become an inexpensive and practical way to share a cable or DSL Internet connection among two or more PCs. More than a third of US homes now have broadband Internet access, and many have two or more PCs. In organizations it lets workers stay on top of e-mail and instant messaging, whether in a conference room down the hall or in a building across campus. Wireless, whether PDA, mobile or Wi-Fi, facilitates shopping and decision-making, reduces sales costs and keeps prospects in the sales cycle. It also helps sales staff and resellers to sell products more effectively.

While wireless enabling sales-force automation applications is a logical step for many companies, doing a thorough step-by-step analysis of a company's sales process may uncover other opportunities for wireless to reduce costs or increase revenues – and not just at the point where salesperson meets potential buyer, but also where products meet shipping dock, and where purchasing meets vendor.

Improving internal communication and operations

Many factors have helped to push wireless where it is now, but the primary one is Wi-Fi (wireless fidelity). While telecommunications companies spent billions in buying up licensed spectrums and struggling to deploy broadband wide-area (3G) networks, the rest of the technology world seized upon this existing wireless local-area networking technology, which roamed unlicensed airwaves, and set to work on expanding its range, speed and capabilities. Wi-Fi use within an organization, even by employees who never leave its facilities, can lower costs, boost productivity and increase flexibility in how various employees carry out their jobs.

Where there is hot-desking and people are rarely at their desks but always on the premises, this is going to be a big contributor to sales of wireless technology.

Wireless can cut the communication delays between members of workgroups that cause lower productivity, late shipments, missed business opportunities, etc. It can improve the management of the contractors and vendors that impact on internal operations. Embedding wireless devices into resources such as vehicles, equipment, assembly lines and software applications can further improve business operations.

How much can your wireless offerings improve a company's internal operations? If you can improve the communication between a brand and its consumers, then maybe you can do the same with its workforce; this then gives you two customers for the price of one.

Chapter 5
Wireless advertising models

Carriers are turning to mobile data services as a new source of revenue and means for increasing ARPU (annual revenue per user). The first thing that any strategist creating a mobile business model must realize is that the economics of packet networks is quite different from that of traditional cellular networks. Cellular networks support only per-minute and flat-rate charging models, while packet-based data networks open the door to a host of new revenue options.

The business models that operators and their partners choose have a high impact on operator-retained revenue streams. Mobile operators are caught between the steady decline of voice ARPU (annual revenue per user) and the cost of upgrading their networks to CDMA2000, GPRS and UMTS.

The mobile operator challenge

The Internet, while a huge 'user' success, was a business failure for the network operators such as Sprint and AT&T. They did not effectively monetize the IP traffic being generated by their customers. The mobile operators cannot afford to have the 'Internet revenue-capture fiasco' happen to them. As a result, operators are under tremendous pressure to figure out a way to share in the value delivered on their mobile networks.

The new revenue models need to address the following:

- a shift from a voice-only, direct relationship with the user to a complex data one
- a move towards a portfolio of enterprise services with multiple partners and revenue sharing

- increased competition, with third parties (MVNOs) also targeting the end-user.

The basic challenge for operators is the integration of the Internet with the mobile, at the device, service and transport levels.

Mobile operator revenue models

The different revenue models for carriers, Mobile Virtual Network Operators (MVNOs) and other access providers (distribution networks) include those listed in Table 5.1.

Killer applications

SMS

Wireless messaging is the number-one driver of data service revenue for wireless carriers, especially European. Europe adopted SMS more quickly because there wasn't the paging network infrastructure that was dominant in the US. SMS can be combined with web technologies to allow advertising on a one-to-one basis. Figure 5.1 illustrates a web-based tool that the well-known fashion brand TONI&GUY used to market a special offer to their customers.

SMS traffic exceeds 25 billion messages per month worldwide, at an average fee of $0.10 per message. SMS messaging is popular in Europe and parts of Asia such as Korea. The big barrier to SMS in the USA has been that, until recently, inter-carrier messaging was not possible. That meant that Cingular users could not send messages to ATT Wireless users, although this is now possible. Cingular says that it has experienced rapid growth in text messaging use, and now handles tens of millions of messages every week.

MMS

MMS builds on familiar text-messaging features, but adds graphics, video, sounds and other multimedia elements. The enhanced messaging service (EMS), a direct descendant of SMS, allows users to send and receive ring tones and operator logos, as well as combinations of simple media, to and from EMS-compliant handsets. The imminent arrival of the MMS infrastructure across networks and the advent of MMS-enabled handsets signals a limited window of opportunity for EMS. MMS offers a logical and lucrative evolution of the short message service (SMS) business model, generating new revenue streams from the existing customer base and luring new customers.

Table 5.1 *Mobile operator revenue models*

Mobile data revenue model	Description	Examples
Session-based charging	Per-minute charges, per-session charges	Linking to multiplayer games, Wi-Fi 802.11b connectivity
Volume-based charging	Per-kilobyte charges	Downloading tunes, downloading music, uploading digital photographs
Per-message (SMS and MMS)	10 cents per minute, 2 cents per minutes with certain packaged deals	Carriers make money from selling airtime
Flat rate per content type	Pay for what you use	No monthly fees, flat rate charging per minute; MobileOne Asia charges 20 cents during peak hours, 10 cents during off-peak hours, and 5 cents after 9 pm and on weekends
Flat rate per content type	'All-you-can-eat' models	SMS messaging, corporate and personal e-mail, instant messaging
Mobile Internet access and basic content subscription services	Portal service (limited number of kilobytes allowed)	America Online; NTT DoCoMo (successful i-mode service charges users a $2.50 monthly fee, plus 25 cents per data packet where one packet is equivalent to 128 bytes of data); Palm.net basic plan (30 messages, 20 stock quotes, 10 sports scores, 10 traffic reports, 10 weather reports)
Mobile Internet access with unlimited or premium content subscription services	Advanced portal services (unlimited kilobytes included in monthly fee)	America Online; Verizon Express Service; Palm.net Unlimited Volume Plan; EarthLink/OmniSky – pricing plan offering Internet service to wireless hand-held computer users for a fee per month
Advertising-based models	Credit for free calls/products in return for watching ads	Vindigo – text-based ads on Palm
Revenue-sharing models	The mobile operator receives a piece of whatever business is generated from a mobile surfer who clicks through a link to a partner site	Under NTT DoCoMo's i-mode model, 91 per cent of revenue from applications goes to developers; in contrast, the best-case revenue sharing scenario in Europe is a 50/50 arrangement between operators and developers.

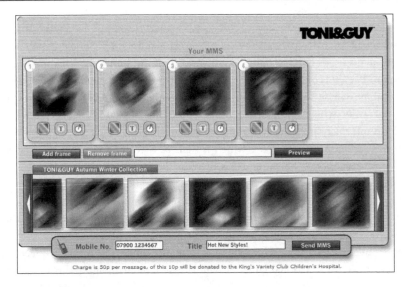

Figure 5.1 *TONI&GUY SMS browser (Sprite Interactive Ltd)*

Advantages of wireless advertising

Wireless advertising is both a reality today and a possibility tomorrow. Right now it is in its infancy, but over the next few years wireless advertising will mature into a more sophisticated, viable medium. One item clearly sets wireless technologies apart from their wired counterparts: mobility. The ability to interact with remote application servers wirelessly from any location allows an individual's location to become an additional, invaluable data point to advertising services.

Wireless advertising has several advantages over other forms of advertising that will make it a hot area in the next few years. Perhaps the most obvious of these is it can reach its audience in a targeted manner when they are out of the office or home. On the most basic level, text sponsorships on text-based wireless sites work in much the same way as other websites. The other primary vehicle, which is available on wireless devices with telephony capability, is spoken audio messages, much like traditional telemarketing.

On the next level there are the possibilities of situational targeting, where targeted advertising would be tailored not just to the habits and preferences of users but also to their location. In the most complete form, situational targeting would allow localized advertising to appear only for those users who meet a pre-defined set of criteria that may include place, time and possibly even activity. These possibilities are very attractive for local advertisers.

The wired world has made great progress in the use of personalization technologies so that appropriate advertisements are targeted to users as they progress through a website. This personalization process can be tailored by adding in the user's location as an additional variable. Instead of being targeted with generic entertainment advertising, a user's wireless phone could instead inform him or her that the nearest Italian restaurant is only two blocks away. If you assume that the next logical step is to combine wireless data, location services and intelligent agents, the day is not very far away when a mobile becomes a 'personal digital assistant'. Currently, location information can only be approximated; the user offers personal information such as a zip or post code, which is then used to send the user ads that are relevant to that code. This method is the basic limit for situational advertising in the foreseeable future. The technology exists physically to track user location at any given moment, but such tracking presents a privacy challenge greater than any of those that Internet advertising is already facing. Many will divulge where they work and live, but it is safe to say that most people would not like to have their every movement tracked. Until there is a mass change in attitude concerning privacy concerns, situational targeting will largely remain an approximate science.

Response rates to mobile campaigns and contests have shown, on average, that:

- 94 per cent of messages are viewed
- 62 per cent of ads are remembered
- 22 per cent of receivers forward offers to friends (viral activity)
- 18 per cent respond to offers.

Currently, SMS has extremely high consumer usage but low business adoption. While billions of SMS messages are delivered between individual consumers each month, the use of SMS as a part of business and marketing strategies is (relatively) low. However, this relatively low business usage is changing rapidly; organizations are beginning to realize the benefits of SMS and are using it as a new medium within their traditional marketing communications strategies. The reason for this increase is that SMS is an extremely cost-effective, high response-rate vehicle that drives loyalty and reinforces branding efforts. Standard communications media available to marketers and advertisers are usually rated on three factors: reach, cost and effectiveness/retention (see Table 5.2).

As a medium newly available, SMS has the following characteristics: high reach, low cost and high retention.

Where does SMS fit in?
WAP, 3G, GPRS and other wireless protocols have each been touted as the next big thing for quite some time, and none have truly materialized. SMS, on the

Table 5.2 *Reach, cost and effectiveness table for communications media*

Medium	Reach	Cost	Effectiveness/retention
Television	Highest	Very high	Good
Radio	Medium	Medium	Poor
Internet (banners)	High	Medium	Dropping
E-mail	High	Extremely low	Extremely low
Print media	Low	High	High
Billboard	Medium	Medium	Medium
POS/POP	Medium	Medium	Medium
Telephone	Medium	High	Medium
Fax	Low	Medium	Low
Direct Mail	High	High	Medium
Personal Interaction	Low	High	High
Wireless SMS	High	Low	High

other hand, has grown of itself into a worldwide phenomenon. For marketing professionals, CRM specialists and business people, there is a great opportunity to harness this medium and be able to serve customers better as a result. Given that SMS has an extremely personal nature (not unlike e-mail), we first have to ensure that we treat the medium with the appropriate level of reverence. How do we go about using this new channel, without making the mistakes that we did with e-mail?

Advertising with bulk SMS

Bulk messaging is when a company sends out a large number of text messages (often hundreds of thousands) to its customer base. For marketing purposes, companies send out content that consumers value and which fits with their brand. In order to do this a company must ensure that it has received phone users' permission to send messages to them. The sender should always clearly identify itself. Examples include:

- 'Pret A Manger – all sandwiches £1 off when you show this message on your phone' Evening Standard
- 'Get into Cinderella's free before 11 pm and Archers 50 p per shot on Thursdays' Cinderella
- 'Get your Party in the Park tickets now on 0870 123456' Capital Radio.

Each message is paid for on a per message basis by the company sending out the messages.

Text message marketing is a very successful and cost-effective way to advertise. The key benefit is that messaging campaigns can be set up at short notice – in under 24 hours. This means they can be used to dispose of unsold inventory.

A further advantage of phone contact is that people have their phones on them all the time, not just at the weekend or at home or at work, so a good offer will reach them wherever they are.

Phone databases can be refreshed at any time by sending out a message – 'Reply to this message to continue to receive future offers' – which means money is not wasted targeting the wrong people.

Despite potential pitfalls, some forms of local advertising may be very lucrative in the future. The Wireless Advertising Industry Association set standard guidelines to apply to this new medium, and at the same time IAB launched a similar effort; they have now merged to form the WAA, or Wireless Advertising Association. They have outlined key initiatives, including:

- ad measurement – defining the metrics and methods for tracking ad delivery and determining ad effectiveness
- creative standards and ad models – defining ad formats and sizes as well as appropriate display methods
- consumer issues and privacy – determining how best to gather consumer acceptance while maintaining consumers' privacy
- ad delivery – determining the processes and associated technology standards for ad delivery.

Most of these are pretty obvious and will probably be worked out independently between advertisers and publishers, but in the long run common standards will be useful.

Regardless of who sets the guidelines, many agree that some standardization is needed for wireless to be a viable advertising medium, and to prevent it from being as unpopular with consumers as telemarketing or the banner. The WAA fight against spam and all forms of push wireless advertising (advertising sent at a time when the user does not issue a request for information) sets the following guidelines:

1 Advertisers and marketers shall not send wireless push advertising and/or content to a subscriber's wireless mobile device without explicit subscriber permission (opt-in). This includes but is not limited to audio, short message

service (SMS), e-mail, multimedia messaging, cell broadcast, picture messages, pushed content or any other 'pushed' advertising and/or content.

2 Subscriber permission for wireless push advertising and/or content must be verified through confirmed opt-in. It is considered the highest level of subscriber permission for e-mail marketing. The WAA expects confirmed opt-in to be the baseline for wireless subscriber permission.

3 Wireless subscriber permission is not transferable to third parties without explicit permission from the subscriber.

4 Clear instructions to unsubscribe (opt-out) must be made readily available to all recipients for all wireless push advertising and/or content and must be honoured.

Advertising convergance

There are other ways in which advertising may emerge. For companies, providing useful information or applications associated with their brand can be beneficial, especially if the users then pass on the information virally, whether informally or by beaming to others. In Asia, some companies offer free or discount wireless phone services for those users willing to listen to short audio ads. In Hong Kong, Peoples Telephone has 88 000 people who have signed up for their mSpot service, which requires users to sit through a short ad before placing a call. For this they get 25 per cent off their bill. Other companies serve their ads intermittently. Singtel, of Singapore, offers free minutes for demographic information.

The wireless advertising pricing methods have yet to be established. Flat rates by the week or month seem to be common; however, there are often per-lead costs built into contracts. Others charge by CPM or CPC. In general there seems to be a lot of flexibility in this space, but as wireless is still somewhat of a novelty and the audience is very skewed to the tech-savvy, this sort of advertising is somewhat expensive. If the aim is to target early adopters, now is the time to implement branding campaigns, as in the future the audience will be less and less targeted. If objectives are direct-response, it may be better to wait. There are currently no third-party tracking systems that offer post-click or post-impression back-end data, so ROI analysis is possible only by employing unique URLs. Sprite Interactive employs this method, but can also capture an e-mail address of a wireless user – invaluable if a company's campaign goal is to drive registrants. In the future there will most likely be more sophisticated tracking methods that will bring wireless tracking up to speed with other Internet tracking, though privacy concerns might keep the cookie at bay for some time.

Dangers to the wireless advertising industry

Although they shouldn't pose a serious threat, it is important to keep the following issues in mind:

1 Litigation in wireless phone cases. This may hurt the industry, but possibly only devices whose interface is phone-like. This may extend to other wireless devices.
2 Laws against cell phone 'spam' – unsolicited messages such as text.
3 Radiation. The industry is now disclosing the amount of radiation emitted from each phone. This could impact on phone use, although probably not significantly if at all.
4 The first wireless virus, 'Timofonica', has already caused problems.
5 Wireless devices will generally have a short range. They will connect to a local network that will translate their requests and actions from wireless to landline protocols, take them to their destination, then reverse the process. Whoever controls these points will be able to charge both ends of the pipe for their services, and will have leverage on everyone involved. How this is going to shake out is very unclear at the moment.

Mobile content

Mobile content providers include Sprite Interactive, Cybird (Japan), Digital Bridges (UK), Disney (US), Infospace (US), iTouch (UK), Ludigames (France), Mforma (US) and Zed (Finland). These companies provide a diverse set of content, including:

1 News. This covers the development and transmission of local, national and international news – society, politics, economics, culture, sports and weather information. It includes alerts, headlines and full articles.
2 Transport information. This encompasses the capture, packaging and transmission of content related to journey planning, incident information and other transportation services such as timetables. It deals with private transport, and short- and long-distance public transport.
3 Financial information. This includes the capture, packaging and distribution of content-related services like stock quotes, exchange rates and analysts' recommendations. These can be text-, audio- or video-based, and in alert or full-article format.
4 Games. This encompasses simple time-killer (Hangman-type) and elaborated applications. Games can be played either online or offline, require a download or not, and be embedded into handsets or not.
5 Edutainment. This contains educational games, interactive reference publications (encyclopedia, dictionaries, etc.) and interactive guides (city guides, museum guides, etc.).

6 Music. This consists of downloading or data-streaming of tracks.
7 Ringing tones and icon downloads.
8 Adult entertainment.
9 Directories.

Note that for each of these applications there are differences in the structure of the market, its business model and the technological requirements to deliver content. However, fundamentally the advertising model is the same for all this content.

Location-based mobile retailing and marketing models

Location infrastructure is just starting to be used by carriers and adopted, but strategic thinking on how to make money from location-based services is still in its infancy. Which wireless location-driven pricing/bundling/couponing strategy should each retailer adopt to attract the customer to their store? Given the limitations of the device and the attention-limited nature of consumer behaviour, what are the effects on mobile retail strategy? How will the customer choose between the competing mobile offers?

Simply providing the location in terms of x and y coordinates isn't enough, though, to kickstart mobile advertising *en masse*. The value of these data lies in tying this information to spatial databases and other information services. Several companies are producing solutions that allow developers to build powerful mobile applications. A number of vendors are marketing server platforms that take location information as an input then output a wide variety of information in a variety of formats. These formats include WAP as well as data to car navigation systems. It is even possible to take things further by offering complete mobile ASP (Application Service Provider) capabilities to mobile operators and carriers. Platforms can utilize a number of advanced, patented algorithms that allow them to determine the *driving* distance, as opposed to the *geographic* distance, to a site.

The next mobile marketing problem is the issue of single product incentives versus bundled product incentives. What bundle of goods should be offered to maximize the chain profits once the customer is inside the store? What is the role of CRM in enabling a sophisticated bundling strategy? How do the strategies change if the customer is a first-time visitor versus a repeat customer versus a loyal customer?

Micropayments and TV voting

It's an understatement to say that expectations for premium SMS are high. Once in place, the service will address the much-touted, but long-undelivered promise of 'micropayments' – those sums of less than a dollar that could, theoretically, be charged for online content, such as viewing individual web pages. Indeed, micropayments are thought of as a way to augment web publishing's slim advertising revenues – perhaps even to the extent of making online publishing profitable. However, because of the transactional costs associated with credit cards, micropayments have so far not been feasible. When premium SMS comes about, it will enable wireless carriers to assume the responsibility for billing.

Premium-rate SMS is the key to making wireless a transactional medium. Internet sites could be the first beneficiaries of this technology – where users have to pay for content, and can pay for it with a mobile phone. Once premium rates come in, this actually becomes a micropayment system. In addition to enabling users to pay for Internet content with their wireless phones, there's no reason why voting-based TV programming can't go premium.

Re-educating the US market

Naturally, there's a hitch with bringing the service to the US. While Europe has been ready, willing and able to send premium SMS messages for some time, US consumers are becoming familiar with standard SMS and its pennies-per-message pricing. As a result, the powers now promoting standard SMS are working hard to get premium SMS up and running. In the US, it's going to be difficult to start to ask customers to pay for it after they have been getting it for free. With money on the line, there's no shortage of players eager to promote the service. Expect networks, publishers and other media partners to be some of the first to get into the act. That's because imposing a premium SMS fee is anticipated to have a dramatic impact on wireless ads – they could suddenly become palatable to cash-strapped advertisers.

Premium SMS also could appeal to television networks because it stands to replace sources of costs with a revenue-generator. While it's now paying 'a very large bill' for the toll-free numbers used during telephone voting, networks would actually make money each time a user voted if they used premium SMS.

With all the money flowing to publishers and advertisers, carriers too will want to be in on the action and are likely to encourage consumers to adopt premium-rate SMS.

Wireless models

Some argue that Wi-Fi and related consumer technologies hold the key to replacing cellular telephone networks such as GSM. Some obstacles to this happening in the near future are absent roaming and authentication features, the narrowness of the available spectrum and the limited range of Wi-Fi. Despite such problems, companies are already offering telephony platforms that use the Wi-Fi backbone.

Many operators are now selling mobile Internet products that link cellular wireless and Wi-Fi radio systems in a more or less transparent way to take advantage of the benefits of both. Future wireless systems are expected routinely to switch between a variety of radio systems. The term '4G' is occasionally used for Wi-Fi, the implication being that the bandwidth and capabilities offered are already greater than those promised by the 3G cellular telephone standards.

The main difference between cellular and Wi-Fi systems is that the cellular system uses the licensed spectrum and Wi-Fi is implemented in unlicensed bands. The economic basis for its implementation is therefore completely different. The success of Wi-Fi has made many people look to the unlicensed spectrum as the future of wireless access, rather than the spectrum licensed and controlled by large corporations.

Wireless is developing in three areas of technology:

1 Local area networks (LAN). A wireless LAN is a network providing wireless peer-to-peer (PC-to-PC, PC-to-hub, or printer-to-hub) and point-to-point (LAN-to-LAN) connectivity within a building or campus. Wireless LANs (WLAN) provide public wireless access to the Internet via 'hot spots'. Hot spots are public spaces, like airports, hotel lounges and cafés, where people can log on to the Internet. WLANs are becoming adopted as unwired warehouses, home, airport Internet access and corporate intranet solutions. The most popular WLANs standard at the moment is 802.11 b, also called Wi-Fi.

2 Personal area networks (PAN). These are based on a global specification, called Bluetooth, which uses radio frequency to transmit voice and data over a short range. Bluetooth is cable-replacement technology that wirelessly synchronizes data across devices and creates transparent access to networks and the Internet. This is ideal for mobile professionals who hate carrying cables and connectors. It helps to link notebook computers, mobile phones, PDAs, PIMs, and other hand-held devices quickly, to do business at home, on the road and in the office. Bluetooth is also a key ingredient of Wearable Computing.

3 Wide area networks (WAN). These utilize digital mobile phone systems – 2.5G or 3G networks – to access data and information from any location in the range of a cell tower connected to a data-enabled network. Using the mobile phone as a modem, a mobile computing device such as a notebook computer, PDA or

Table 5.3 *Wireless revenue models*

Revenue model	Description	Examples/usage
Monthly subscription service	Individuals, corporations, educational institutions, and federal, state and local governments for Internet or secure intranet access	Metricom (bankrupt); MobileStar (bankrupt); Waypoint; Boingo Wireless
Pay per use	Downloads of information and entertainment, or purchase of Internet time	Any consumer entertainment company offering music, video, games; local real-estate agents
Premium surcharge for wireless subscribers	Enhanced connection speeds for heavy data users	Mobile operators, PDA vendors offering wireless connectivity, paging networks
Advertising-supported	Downloads with advertisements, access points to attract public to promotional displays or retail stores	Maps for free download at airports with local business advertising; access points on billboards or in shopping malls
Free to users (company-wide infrastructure or home infrastructure)	Company-wide intra-firewall use for all mobile employees on a campus; home usage with a set-top box acting as a Wi-Fi gateway	Conference/meeting rooms/classrooms; warehouses; manufacturing floor; e-mail use

device with a stand-alone radio card can receive and send information from a network, corporate intranet or the public Internet.

Revenue models

Revenue models are listed in Table 5.3.

Nokia Wi-Fi strategy

Nokia has launched a new PC card that connects notebooks to wireless data networks. The new card, the Nokia D211, is compatible with both GPRS and 802.11-b wireless networks. Laptop users within around 100 metres (328 feet) of a WLAN site and with the right set-up on their computer can get access to the Internet and their own secure corporate network at speeds of up to 500 kbps.

Summary

The advertising opportunities that exist are global. From all indications, Europe (Scandinavia), Asia (especially Japan) and the US will be the primary markets. There is a widely shared misconception that all a site has to do is add a wireless protocol to their bag of tricks and they can support wireless. Those looking into this point out that the sites will have to undergo massive redesign or bring up secondary sites in order really to support wireless. The Japanese model is usually cited, as this has tailored both site design and content to support wireless. While opportunities will be increasing in other countries, overall these consumer markets will remain relatively small for the near future.

Chapter 6
Delivering content to wireless devices

Ask many in the mobile phone industry what will keep the revenue of the main operators growing in the coming years, and you just might hear 'content, content, content'. Paradoxically this is also the biggest challenge for service providers as, no matter how good the content, if it is not distributed effectively it is unlikely to catch the eye of consumers – and if they can't see it, they simply can't buy it. The content market is currently flourishing, with the Wireless World Forum predicting that the mobile games market will climb to $1.93 billion in 2006, so the opportunity to make money from mobile content is there – but how do you take advantage of it, and how do you get your content delivered to the user's mobile device?

Working with mobile operators and aggregators to deliver your content

You must first consider all possible routes to market, including mobile operators, aggregators, device manufacturers, consumer-facing portals and more. While going directly to your mobile operator of choice might seem the most obvious route to success, it may not be effective or even realistic. Mobile operators have a limited number of resources, and many have decided to focus their efforts on branded content which already has brand recognition. The difficulty of building a direct relationship with operators should not act as a deterrent; there are more and more developer channels opening up, and many operators now rely on outside parties to source content. An interesting model is the tiered access system, with different developers accessing operators in different ways. O2, in the UK, has a three-tier strategy when it comes to mobile games and other applications. It works directly with tier-one developers to create O2-branded content, then with tier-two developers to deliver partner-branded content. Third-tier developers can access

O2 through a dedicated developer program called Revolution. Working on a tiered basis has its rewards but also its setbacks – the third parties who work with operators usually demand a cut of the revenue on content sold, and may demand membership fees; however, they do have a wealth of knowledge of the market, and can provide you with a valuable 'foot in the door'. There is a number of questions to bear in mind when discussing content distribution agreements with an operator or aggregator, including the following:

1 What is the submission process for my content?
2 Are there fees involved?
3 How long does it typically take to get content to market?
4 How will my content be priced?
5 How will my content be promoted or marketed?
6 Where will my content be placed in the overall content directory?
7 What tracking and reporting facilities are there (is there real-time download tracking)?
8 How will I get paid for content downloads?

Each operator or aggregator will have specific technical requirements that you will need to work to, and you'll need to consider things like handset compatibility, which assets you need to supply (screengrabs, marketing text, etc.), style compliance, testing requirements and certification requirements. Some operators even require that applications go through third-party screening and certification processes, or be qualified on specific devices – such as Nokia, which requires all Java content to be 'Java verified' before allowing it to be featured on their software marketplace. This can be costly. You may also want to consider approaching handset manufacturers directly. Many developers, such as Samsung, have their own content portals, which receive a lot of traffic (Figure 6.1).

Web portals are another great route to market, and tend to be more willing to accept new content than are operators. New content services are springing up that provide consumers with the ability to purchase content by providing all of the purchase and billing capabilities as well as the over-the-air (OTA) delivery mechanisms to deliver the content to the user's phone from the web; however, you will find that the revenue share you receive from web portals will tend to be lower than that from operators.

Other distribution channels

Both wireless operators and content providers now have to consider the full range of content distribution channels available. Today, wireless operators have become the main channel for distributing content onto mobile devices. Not only

Figure 6.1 *The Handyx website www.handyx.net*

can end-users easily access wireless content anytime and anywhere, but they also have an established billing relationship already in place with their wireless operator. There are, however, many other distribution channels available that provide realistic ways for content developers and distributors to reach the phone user.

One of the main drivers for this growth in distribution channels is the rapid expansion of storage capacity, which is growing cheaper and cheaper. It is rational to think that the average size of wireless content will continue to grow, with full-length movies and large games becoming available. However, the data transfer speeds are not following quite the same trend. Whilst the lead from 2.5G to 3G has given a large speed improvement, it is still not going to keep up with the growth in handset storage capacity, which is predicted to triple by 2007. This leads to the conclusion that wireless operators and content developers will embrace high-capacity distribution channels such as cartridges.

The main hand-held device to use cartridges so far is the N-Gage, which was greeted with mixed reactions. There are two types of development that can occur for an N-Gage – J2ME development and cartridge game development. If you want to develop a game or other application that can be downloaded, you'll want to use J2ME. The N-Gage supports J2ME by using Java MIDP, and has the same architecture as mobile phone. To make the N-Gage a proper games machine, and in an attempt to enter it into the same league as the Nintendo Gameboy, Nokia also added support for MultiMedia Cartridges (MMC). As with other gaming systems, these are the game cartridges you buy and use with the system. These applications are created using C++ for the Symbian operating system. In order to build the MMC cartridge solutions, you need to use the N-Gage SDK that builds on the Series 60 platform and SDK from Nokia. The main problem with the cartridge functionality on the original N-Gage was that to change games the user had to take the back cover of the handset off and remove the battery, which is an awkward process at the best of times. However, this has been resolved in the latest N-Gage update.

One company that has started retailing Symbian games on MMCs is The Carphone Warehouse. This has set a potential new trend for other companies to follow, which would turn in even more capital as mobile games become more popular. Each MMC card includes three titles: Marble Revolution, winner of the Best Gaming Application in the Nokia 2005 Series 60 Challenge; Sky Force, a critically-acclaimed, fast-paced arcade shoot 'em up; and Yukiko, an arcade puzzler, which combines the action and strategy of old-school classics such as Bomberman* and Sokoban*. All three titles have scored very highly in the games press and have already built up an enthusiastic fan-base around the world. This kind of cartridge-based gaming has worked well for Nintendo with the Gameboy, but the same cannot be said for Nokia; however, the MMC is a great way to distribute content. There is a lot of space on an MMC, and this can be filled with a variety of content rather than just a game. It could, for example, be packed with wallpapers, ring tones or phone themes, and these could be related to a game sold on the MMC or as a 'wallpaper pack' or 'ring-tone pack' – a great way to distribute a lot of content on one delivery device.

Another area that is taking advantage of using MMCs to deliver content is the film industry. Rok Entertainment was the first UK-based company to launch feature films on MMC cartridges, in January 2005. The movies come packaged in multimedia cards (MMC), the format being compatible with secure digital (SD) slots. They also include a media player that formats the film for the phone screen. It remains to be seen how successful these films will be, but with a high selling price (around £15 each) and the limitations of the small screen their appeal is limited.

Point-of-sale delivery

Retail stores are only just starting to catch up with mobile content, and have been pretty much left behind in a world that has so far dealt with over-the-air delivery. Some solutions have been commercialized, such as scratch cards, which enable users to download content via a Premium SMS service. However, nowadays, as more and more smartphones embed removable storage capabilities such as MMCs, retail stores are expected to take advantage of the evolution. This is already the case with the Nokia N-Gage, as mentioned previously. Many customers prefer to buy content in a physical sense, and this is the advantage that retail outlets have. Shops such as newsagents and petrol stations are increasingly selling boxed mobile games that contain codes for the user to text in; this then triggers the download of the game to their phone. Although not a truly 'physical' game, it goes some way to achieving this.

Ki-Bi

One interesting and quite novel use of point-of-sale material has been developed by a company called Ki-Bi, which produces credit-card sized cards with buttons on them (Figure 6.2). The user dials a number and presses a button on the card for the content they want to download. The card plays a tune into the handset, which then triggers delivery of the content to the user's handset. The content comes in as an SMS containing a WAP link straight to the content. The beauty of this system is that users can swap cards, so they become like collection cards, and users are charged directly on their bill with the premium SMS.

Wireless file transfer

Technology that allows your computer or phone to communicate with other devices wirelessly can free your home of cables and wires, and is a great way to get content onto handsets. There are two main wireless transfer technologies in use; Bluetooth and infrared.

Smart Technology enables Simple Operation

The user friendly activation is achieved by the proprietary sophisticated technology behind it

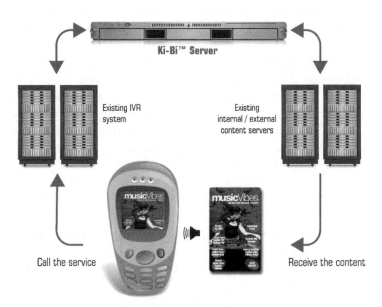

Figure 6.2 *Ki-Bi system architecture – reproduced with permission*

Bluetooth

Bluetooth is an alliance between mobile communications and mobile computing companies to develop a short-range communications standard allowing wireless data communications at ranges of about 10 metres, and was originally conceived by Ericsson in 1994, when they began a study to examine alternatives to cables that linked mobile phone accessories. Ericsson already had a strong capability in short-range wireless, and they used this knowledge to develop the specification for Bluetooth wireless. Bluetooth technology is an 'enabling technology'; it is designed to be incorporated in a very wide range of products to allow them to intercommunicate. Bluetooth is now built into many new notebook and hand-held systems, desktop computers, mobile phones and even printers as standard these days, and will allow you to connect devices over short distances and transfer data between them as and when you need to. Bluetooth is named after a King – Harald Blat, translated as Bluetooth in English. Bluetooth was first introduced in 1998, and uses radio waves to transmit wireless data over short distances. Bluetooth can support many users in any environment.

Bluetooth is a radio-based technology that allows devices to share information over a maximum range of 100 metres. The beauty of Bluetooth is that, unlike other wireless technologies such as infrared, the devices don't need to be pointing at each other; they can make a connection as long as they are in range of one another. You can, for example, use a Bluetooth headset with a Bluetooth-enabled mobile phone that is stashed in your pocket, or use a Bluetooth printer with a Bluetooth laptop. With Bluetooth, you can also transfer your content between a PC and a mobile phone or hand-held computer via OBEX (a communications protocol that facilitates the exchange of binary objects between devices). This is a great way to get content onto a mobile device in a quick and easy manner. It is also possible to synchronize data wirelessly between a desktop and a hand-held computer if both are Bluetooth-enabled. It is worth remembering, though, that Bluetooth can be a real drain on battery-powered devices such as mobile phones and hand-held computers, so your best bet is to turn Bluetooth on only when you need it, leaving it switched off when you don't.

In summary, Bluetooth has a number of applications:

1 Wireless networking between desktops and laptops, and peripherals such as printers and keyboards
2 Transfer of files (images, MP3s, etc.) between mobile phones, PDAs and computers via OBEX
3 Bluetooth headsets for mobile phones.

Bluetooth technology has a lot of potential and is continuing to change. Many revisions have been carried out, and more are expected. The specification of the technology has been widely accepted by leading industries. The possibility of the emergence of new applications using Bluetooth is high, and the technology is expected to be used in many other advanced applications in the near future.

You can check out more information about Bluetooth on the Bluetooth Special Interest Group website, www.bluetooth.com.

IrDA infrared

Infrared is one of the most longstanding and popular wireless communication technologies, it first gained popularity in the home entertainment industry, where television, VCRs and stereos could be controlled via a remote wireless device that beamed information across a room to a unit. Infrared can send information over a distance of up to 2 metres, although shorter distances of 20–30 centimetres consume much less power. IrDA infrared is different than the TV remote control. TV IR uses commands and controls to send a small amount of data and is one way. IrDA transmits data at up to 16 Mbps and is two way. The standard distance is 1 metre even though depending on the transceivers, it can be longer. Infrared has become popular primarily because it is relatively inexpensive to install. Infrared is not only an ideal content transfer technology, its presence in most

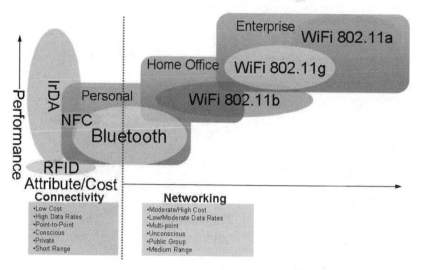

Wireless Technologies

Figure 6.3 *Wireless Technology Relationships – courtesy of the IrDA*

consumer devices also makes it an ideal technology for transmitting payment information. Although the line-of-sight requirements of infrared are a disadvantage for some applications, consumers and merchants may be reassured that payment information is not being intercepted, as they must be face-to-face to complete a transaction.

Infrared devices usually conform to standards published by the Infrared Data Association (IrDA; Figure 6.4). IrDA devices use infrared light-emitting diodes (LEDs) to emit infrared radiation, which is focused by a plastic lens into a narrow beam; this is modulated to encode the data. The receiver uses a silicon photodiode to convert the infrared radiation to an electric current. It responds only to the rapidly pulsing signal created by the transmitter, and filters out slowly changing infrared radiation from ambient light. To transmit content between phones or an infrared-enabled computer and a handset, you have to activate the infrared on both devices. When the infrared icon stays solid, it is an indication that you are transferring data back and forth. Red lights are only with TV remotes. With phones or PDAs you will not see a red light. The user will see icons on the phone/PDA display that let you know that data is being sent. Infrared has been used in a number of multiplayer games, but its use as a data and content transfer tool is generally limited compared to Bluetooth by the fact that devices have to be facing each other for the transmission to take place. Infrared is, however, much more applicable as a payment method.

Figure 6.4 *The IrDA website, http://www.irda.org – reproduced with permission*

Delivering content to a BlackBerry®

Online distribution has proved itself to be an important delivery channel for the mobile content industry. In the online mobile content area, many consider Handango to be a success story – particularly their BlackBerry content, which is a great example of a desktop delivery environment as opposed to an over-the-air model. The BlackBerry has been developed by the Canadian company RIM to be the only portable e-mail, Internet and personal information management system that you need, and through clever marketing RIM has managed to make the BlackBerry the essential business handset. The BlackBerry Desktop Manager software allows you to synchronize your BlackBerry with your PC, and deliver applications to the handset via USB. While the software is easy to use and install, this transfer method is quite long-winded and has the additional overhead of having to set up extra software on your PC and plug in cables for the data transfer. Handango is introducing over-the-air delivery for the BlackBerry, which is a much more viable and user-friendly mechanism. If you are planning on developing applications for the BlackBerry, it is now important to consider both OTA delivery and desktop delivery to cater for the maximum number of users.

Wi-Fi – a different perspective on content delivery

Wi-Fi is short for 'Wireless Fidelity', and is a set of product compatibility standards for wireless local area networks based on the IEEE 802.11 specifications. Wi-Fi was intended to be used in mobile devices and local area networks, but is now often used for Internet access. It enables a person with a Wi-Fi-enabled computer or PDA to connect to the Internet when in proximity to an access point, which is also called a hot spot. Because of the nature of Wi-Fi, it can also be used for a range of data and content transfer applications; you can transfer data from a computer to a mobile handset, for example. The next generation of mobile handsets will have Wi-Fi built in as standard, to allow you to use them as wireless modems. Commercial Wi-Fi services are available in a variety of places, including cafés, hotels and airports around the world, and free Wi-Fi services are increasingly being offered by businesses and universities.

The Wi-Fi Alliance

The Wi-Fi Alliance is an industry organization committed to promoting the growth of wireless Local Area Networks (WLANs), with the aim of enhancing user experience for mobile wireless devices. They have developed a number of testing and certification programs to ensure that products based on the IEEE 802.11 specification can operate together. Their logo is a seal of quality on any Wi-Fi product.

Wi-Max and Wi-Bro – the future of Wi-Fi?

Wi-Max and Wi-Bro have been touted as the next generation of wireless networking technology. They offer much faster speeds and longer ranges than standard Wi-Fi. Wi-Max and Wi-Bro are based on different versions of the same basic standard, IEEE 802.16. Wi-Max is designed to send a signal of several tens of megabits per second to fixed receivers over a distance of several tens of kilometres, while Wi-Bro is aimed at sending a 1-Mbps signal to receivers moving at speeds of up to 70 kilometres per hour.

These technologies have the potential to enable millions more to access the Internet wire-lessly, cheaply and easily, with wireless distances measured in kilo-metres as opposed to the metres of Wi-Fi. The technology also provides shared data rates up to 70 Mbps, which should be enough bandwidth to supply around a thousand homes with 1-Mbps DSL-level connectivity. As well as simple connectivity Wi-Max has a number of other interesting potential uses, such as gaming, with Microsoft currently considering integrating it into their XBox 360 console. The potential for gamers to join local networks to play online, without the latency associated with Internet access, must surely be appealing to many gamers.

Intel – the developers of Wi-Max – and the Korean developers of the Wi-Bro system have ensured that the two will work together into the future, and it is predicted that Wi-Bro networks will roll out in 2006. The portability of Wi-Bro combined with the speed and range of Wi-Max promises exciting developments in the future, and it will be fascinating to see how the integration of each technology into wireless devices will shape the future of communications.

Chapter 7

M-commerce

M-commerce (mobile commerce) is the buying and selling of goods and services through wireless hand-held devices such as cellular telephones, personal digital assistants (PDAs) and wireless computers. 3G has opened up the wireless world because of its portability and bandwidth, making computers the one of the most popular devices for data transfer. Known as next-generation e-commerce, m-commerce enables users to access the Internet without needing to find a place to plug in. The emerging technology behind m-commerce, which is based on the Wireless Application Protocol (WAP), has made far greater strides in Europe, where mobile devices equipped with web-ready micro-browsers are much more common than in the United States.

The beauty of WAP is that it is supported by all operating systems (devices include PalmOS, EPOC, Windows CE, FLEXOS, OS/9 and Java OS). WAP devices that use displays and access the Internet run what are called micro–browsers – browsers with small file sizes that can accommodate the low memory constraints of hand-held devices and the low-bandwidth constraints of a wireless-hand-held network. Although WAP supports HTML and XML, the WML language (an XML application) is specifically devised for small screens and one-hand navigation without a keyboard. WAP also supports WMLScript. It is similar to JavaScript, but makes minimal demands on memory and CPU power because it does not contain many of the unnecessary functions found in other scripting languages.

As the range of billing systems is made more available, freedom of choice for the end-user is growing. However, with this greater freedom of choice comes added complexity. Each different business model has its own marketing methods, and technical issues and constraints. As the mobile market has matured and become more structured and open, we can identify three main billing models that have appeared:

1 The standard model is one in which the content or service provider actually incurs a cost, which must then be recouped by other means using another billing support. A company that sends direct marketing messages to its customers pays for all the messages it sends. If the client sends a reply, it's the client who pays to send that message.

2 The premium model is a revenue-producing model in which the content or service provider earns money from its service. The user pays for a service at a pre-defined price – in other words, the mobile 'pays for itself'. In this model, however, the operators keep the lion's share of the profits. SMS was the first to offer an efficient and complete business model for billing solutions, both for standard and premium offers. The success of the SMS model paved the way for new channels like mobile browsing.

3 The traditional model is used where the mobile market has opened up to the Internet world. This new model allows content and service providers to make use of traditional billing supports, often bypassing the operators completely.

The standard model

The standard model consists of billing the sender of a message, whether the sender is an end-user (a mobile-originated, or MO, message) or a service provider (mobile-terminate, or MT, message). This model is used for SMS and MMS messaging.

Standard MO messages

Operators are waging a real price war on the price of SMS MOs. It is often difficult to work out how much a single message actually costs, since many operators offer packages of 30, 100, 200 or even an unlimited amount of SMS messages for a set price each month. The only thing that is clear is that prices are coming down. It costs between two and three times as much to send an MO to an international mobile phone number, however. In that case, additional charges are tacked on for operator network connection fees.

Standard MT messages

Many companies use messaging as an efficient way to communicate with their employees and customers. The fee for this traffic is calculated at a discount, volume-based rate. The price of an SMS MT message varies depending on message volume and where the messages are routed. SMS MTs can also be sent abroad, using either mobile operators or third-party access providers. Mobile operators often apply high interconnection fees, whereas access providers can provide low prices for direct connections.

Billing for standard browsing

In general, browsing a non-premium site on a mobile phone is free, no matter how often or for how long you visit the site. End-users pay a fee for their high-speed GPRS/UMTS connection, but on the whole these costs are relatively minor. The content provider gets nothing for creating this service.

The premium model

The premium model has been around since 1998, with the arrival of SMS technology to the Scandinavian markets. Premium SMS has been widely used throughout Europe because it was a key factor in the success of SMS services in Europe; it has been adopted and adapted to mobile browsing and, to a lesser extent, MMS. The premium model always follows two main principles:

1 Premium fee. The end-users pay a premium fee to view value-added services on their mobiles. The fee is included on the bill from their network operator. Operators usually offer a number of pre-defined service packages.
2 Revenue-sharing. Revenues generated by premium fees are shared between several parties, including mobile operators, and service and content providers. This is how third parties are able to generate revenues and build a successful business model.

Users can be billed for premium messaging, either when they request a service (premium MO) or when they receive a service (premium MT).

Premium MT

Premium MT is ideal for delivering content such as logos or ring tones, as well as subscription-based services such as sports and news alerts, horoscopes, jokes, stock quotes and so on.

Premium MO

This services users' requests for special content or services like TV voting, multimedia content, gaming, competitions, chat and dating services and so on. The type of service offered by the operator directly affects the kind of premium services that can be launched. Premium MT creates more business than premium MO, as long as operators clearly define their subscription terms and the way for users to opt-out.

Billing for premium browsing

The browsing offer in itself does not include a billing model – browsing is just a way to view information presented on a website. Operators therefore either redevelop their own billing system (like W-HA in France) or use the premium SMS model as a way to bill for the service.

Theoretically, there are three types of billing models for premium browsing:

1 Pay per kb, where users are charged for the quantity of content downloaded usually through WAP browsing. Operators rarely share revenues on this fee, considering it a 'transport' charge with no added value.
2 Pay per subscription, where users are charged a subscription fee to access a site. The fee is for a pre-defined period (day, week, month) or for a maximum number of credit uses. This model has the advantage of convincing end-users to visit the site on a regular basis, since they do not have to pay for each individual visit.
3 Pay per use, where users pay each time they use a service or download content. This is the most frequently used model. It provides clear visibility with regard to the price end-users pay for the service, but doesn't help to convince them to use the service on a regular basis.

Traditional billing models

Traditional billing models of charging for goods and services can also be used to bill for mobile services and content. They have become more relevant as the wireless industry opens up to the Internet world. These traditional billing models are often used on standard websites, and can be easily applied to mobile browsing. Companies manage their own billing and account systems independently from operators. These payment methods follow the same basic principles as the premium model: phone users pay a fee that is shared amongst several parties. However, clients are not billed on their mobile phone invoice; they are billed directly to their bank or credit card, or simply purchase a prepaid card.

Some of these supports include:

1 Credit cards, where users pay with their regular credit card to subscribe to value-added mobile phone services

2 Prepaid/scratch cards, where users buy a card with a number of prepaid units that can be used to pay for mobile services

3 IVR, where, instead of sending a text message, users call a premium phone number.

Industries affected by m-commerce

In order to exploit the m-commerce market potential, handset manufacturers such as Nokia, Ericsson, Motorola and Qualcomm have worked with carriers such as AT&T Wireless and Sprint to develop WAP commerce-enabled smart phones. In addition, Wi-Fi and Bluetooth technologies offer an alternative to the mobile operator networks but can use the underlying WAP interface. (There is more about these technologies in Chapter 6.) Smart phones offer fax, e-mail and phone capabilities all in one, paving the way for m-commerce to be accepted by an increasingly mobile workforce.

As content delivery over wireless devices becomes faster, more secure, and scalable, m-commerce will surpass online e-commerce as the method of choice for digital commerce transactions. The industries affected by m-commerce include financial services, information services, the service and retail sectors, and telecommunications.

Financial services

Financial services includes mobile banking (when customers use their hand-held devices to access their accounts and pay their bills) as well as brokerage services, in which stock quotes can be displayed and trading conducted from the same hand-held device. The financial services industry is best placed to exploit advances in mobile technology, this is because its products are totally intangible, and do not need to be physically delivered to consumers. Online e-commerce has been embraced by 'traditional' financial service providers for two main reasons. The first (and most frequently documented) reason is the potential cost savings that it provides. The second, and perhaps more important, factor is the rapidly growing number of financial consumers with access to new media channels. For these institutions, wireless commerce is just the next step.

Information services

Information services include the delivery of financial news, sports figures and traffic updates to a single mobile device. The US is normally a good year ahead of Europe when it comes to the adoption of new technology, but there is one area where the Europeans are way ahead: the use of cell phones to access information services over the Internet. North America is about to follow suit. One early proponent of offering news via WAP is the UK newspaper *The Guardian* (http://www.newsunlimited.com). *The Guardian*'s web service strategy is all about offering readers access to its news, wherever they are, through whatever device they own. *The Guardian* service is totally ubiquitous. It is clear that the customers using these information services and accessing the Internet by WAP phone are very different in profile from PC users. They don't have a fixed profile of being at home or at work, and this difference was taken into consideration when developing *The Guardian*'s WAP content.

The service and retail sectors

Mobile commerce technology is allowing for new communications among retailers, customers, employees and suppliers at the point of need – anytime, any place. Retailers already have begun to conceptualize and implement comprehensive m-commerce strategies. Customers and employees can reduce the amount of time spent in the back office doing administrative work, such as checking inventory.

In the near future, innovative retailers will be able to revolutionize their customers' shopping experience by making purchases easier, timelier and more convenient. A consumer sitting at home reading the Sunday paper could soon scan an ad with a cell phone or PDA to make an impulse purchase. A customer could receive an alert that the shoes he or she expressed an interest in have just gone on sale. A salesperson assisting a shopper could readily suggest some complementary items because the individual's purchase history is in a PDA in his or her hand.

Telecommunications

Telecommunications is probably the most obvious sector opening up the mobile device as a tool to handle bills and all the administrative issues, including service changes, bill payment and account reviews. These can all be conducted from the same hand-held device.

The mobile commerce revolution

Japan has pioneered the mobile commerce revolution ahead of the US and Europe. The Japanese love of gadgetry has been the main driver behind this revolution, but analysts also attribute the phenomenal success to the mobile Internet, in particular the i-mode service. Estimates suggest that recession-ridden Japan is two years ahead of the rest of the world. So what is the secret of its m-commerce success? In Japan, $400m worth of m-commerce revenues are generated annually, and NTT DoCoMo's i-mode service has over 13 million subscribers.

NTT DoCoMo is the world's second largest mobile phone operator, and a subsidiary of telecoms giant NTT. Such is the success of its mobile Internet offering that US Internet giant AOL struck a deal with DoCoMo and took control of its Japanese subsidiary to control the i-mode service.

NTT DoCoMo's success is attributed to the sending and receiving of e-mail as part of the package. This service allows users to send and receive e-mail, and gives them access to more than 7000 Internet sites, via their mobile phones.

The carriers in Japan took risks based on the assumption that the Japanese would be able to embrace these technologies, and created more powerful applications than we see here in Europe. The strategy was simple: once critical mass is achieved, more content will arrive; and the more content received, the more mass is developed. Crucial to this success was that NTT and KDDI – another Japanese carrier – offered packet data networks, which makes sure that customers only pay when they send and receive data.

The growth outside Japan

Carriers outside Japan have tried to limit the users' experience to a 'walled garden'. Just like the walled-garden services sold by Internet ISP many years ago, this has definitely stifled growth. We should view these services first as growing the market, not keeping people contained in a small garden. Walling your users does not encourage content providers to do business with the carriers.

France's Bouygues Telecom has successfully duplicated the Japanese wireless experience. In November 2003, a year after the launch, Bouygues upgraded its i-mode service by launching Java application download sites. DoCoMo had done the same in Japan 23 months after i-mode's start there. Java-based content started with several dozen applications on tap, including games and maps, and could be accessed via the new Java-compliant NEC N341i and Mitsubishi M341i i-mode handsets. These offered much-improved features over the earlier i-mode models, including 65 356-colour and 262 000-colour displays, cameras, 40-voice polyphonic ring-tone capability, and expanded memory for storing photos, messages and address book entries.

Bouygues Telecom has invested a great deal of energy into fostering a content developer community – perhaps more so than DoCoMo has in Japan, where other carriers have also helped to develop the mobile Internet and Java developer community. They put a lot of effort into training content providers and leading them to produce very good i-mode sites, with strict usability guidelines.

Prior to the French mobile carrier Bouygues Telecom launching i-mode, data services in Europe's largest country were weak – and with KPN's i-mode already struggling next door in Holland, Belgium and Germany, i-mode's French prospects were not so strong. France already had its famous Minitel system, wedded to fixed-line terminals in consumers' homes. France's i-mode has taken off due largely to the arrival of better handsets similar to those in Japan, a tight i-mode marketing focus, and an emphasis on a well-defined and controlled portal strategy, all copied faithfully from DoCoMo in Japan.

Early German, Dutch and Belgian i-mode services suffered from poor-quality handsets that, at least initially, didn't even come close to the highly advanced models available in Japan. There was no i-mode-enabled cell phone available from dominant European leader Nokia when KPN's i-mode started, so frustrated KPN customers had to make do with recycled discards from Japanese makers – like NEC's N21i, a 120-gram beast with an uninspiring 256-colour display. Mitsubishi and Toshiba later fielded i-mode handsets for Europe.

Paying the bill

As i-mode was easy to charge, content providers were further motivated to tailor their service to suit this system. NTT DoCoMo upgraded its billing system so costs for premium services, such as news in English from CNN, can be added to a user's phone bill. The carriers make money in two ways: they charge users for the volume of data transmitted over the packet data network, and they make revenues from services that use their billing systems. NTT's clear position as leader of a slowly-opening market gave it a strong position in talks with manufacturers, and it was able to stipulate the design of handsets to hardware vendors. The European and US carriers may offer voice handsets with a browser attached, but NTT worked with vendors to design handsets optimized for data.

European carriers have paid hand over fist for third-generation mobile phone licences, which few are convinced will provide a return on their investment. For NTT, the m-commerce gamble has paid off. Earlier this year, when NTT unveiled its results, its bumper profits were linked to the m-commerce boom, in the face of declining profits in a saturated voice telephony market.

In the UK, Orange has spent £4.09 billion on its licence; in Germany, its affiliate Mobilcom spent £5.19 billion. Analysts say that Orange has forked out for a telephone bill of over £11.5 billion. In fact, most of the winners now have an unhealthy amount of debt on their balance sheets, which has made investors a bit edgy in recent months. For example, British Telecommunication's quest for a 3G licence has played a large part in contributing to the company's £30 billion debt. Similarly, France Telecom (which owns 85 per cent of Orange) and Telecom Italia have ended up with debts of €19 billion and €70 billion respectively. In Holland, KPN has also been hit hard by its €8.85 billion investment in 3G, which has pushed its overall debt up to €22 billion.

3G licence holders need to take into account the threat of competing technologies. With such a large potential market up for grabs, competition is likely to be fierce. The threat of competing technologies to 3G is obvious. EDGE and Wi-Fi offering 400 kbps to mobile handsets could undermine the business prospects of 3G. The current licence holders have now realized that investment is necessary to tackle any threat to 3G. Telecoms giant Orange has already arranged contracts worth £1.42 billion with mobile equipment makers in the UK, Germany and France. These include deals worth £930 million with Nokia, £310 million with Ericsson and £186 million with Alcatel. Orange has floated itself on the stock market to arrange credit worth 150 per cent of the equipment contracts' value. This will take the overall borrowing power of Orange to £3.45 billion and greatly enhance its ability to invest heavily in 3G technology.

Ironically, whilst sceptics are already writing off mobile commerce, a large part of the population doesn't know what it is. For those who don't, the simple answer is that it allows you access to some Internet services and to carry out some transactions on your mobile phone. For those that do know, the message is, it will get better.

In Japan, i-mode is big largely because it is cheap, fast and offers access to about 700 official sites and thousands of unofficial sites. Users can send e-mails, transfer funds between bank accounts, book plane tickets, find the nearest hotel or restaurant, play interactive games, check their horoscope and download melodies. Will it or a similar service be big here? In theory, it should be – if the lessons of Japanese success are followed. Bigger and better screens, more choice of content and, finally, more secure networks are needed.

No one in Japan, or anywhere else in the world, likes to input words using the numeric keypad on the telephone. This is a complaint heard in every country where m-commerce is being attempted. At least in Japan the screens are dramatically different from even those at the cutting edge in Europe and North America – they are larger, have higher resolution and use colour. However, still everybody complains about the low resolution and the size of the screen. You cannot do much on these screens, and colour does not really help enough to make up for the poor resolution. For m-commerce to be successful, the challenge for mobile device manufacturers and the service and content providers is to make the screens bigger and with higher resolution.

A superficial view of the Japanese market shows that users are buying a lot on their phones and that sales continue to increase, but if you examine what the Japanese are buying you will realize that they are not that far ahead of the rest of the world. They are buying predominantly screen-savers and new ringing tones. Compared to current mobile transactions elsewhere in the world, that is a lot of commerce. Other servicers do exist, but generally the take-up has not been so high. We are told that auction-type products and theatre tickets do well, but when you look at the figures and speak to the users it is, inevitably, clear that all these processes have been initiated on a PC. In the auction case, users check the progress of the auction and bid when necessary. In most cases, that is on their PC at work.

Revenue models

The different revenue models for content providers – creators, syndicators and packagers – include licensing, referrals and transactions. There are many other digital content revenue models, including one-time access fees, time-of-usage in any increment, peak/off-peak times, and per item based pricing (see Table 7.1).

Wi-Fi

The hype surrounding deployment of Wi-Fi as a competitor to 3G services is justified because Wi-Fi has revolutionized networking on desktops and laptops. The things that have always stood in the way of hand-held devices are Wi-Fi chip power consumption and the lack of innovation in battery life. On most consumer devices employing embedded Wi-Fi chips, battery life has been dismal. For a Wi-Fi phone device to be palatable to the market, we will need to see a usable battery life of 24 hours at least – rather than the current 2 hours. The great thing about Wi-Fi is that it uses the Internet as its medium for delivering content.

Other wireless processing methods

M-commerce first started with the use of wireless POS (Point-Of-Sale) swipe terminals, and has since then made its way into cellular phones and PDAs (Personal Digital Assistants). Wireless POS swipe terminals are much more expensive than

Table 7.1 Revenue models for content providers

Mobile content revenue model	Description	Examples
Pay per use	Every time someone uses the content through a portal, the content providers get a cut of typically 50–90 per cent	Cybird (Japan); Infospace; i-mode; Vodafone Live
Recurring flat fee xubscription	Unlimited usage included in hourly, daily, weekly or monthly fee	Cybird (Japan); Bango; Endemol
Revenue-sharing models	The mobile operator receives a piece of whatever business was generated by a mobile surfer who clicked through a link to a partner site	Java sales of games on portals; content providers doing business on or through the mobile portal are looking for true sales and distribution channels
Time-specific pricing	Content available at a specific price point for a limited period	Short-term promotions, such as airline or concert tickets – e.g. Ticketmaster, Expedia
Personalized services and content	Pricing based on personalization	Mobile phones have unique IDs and, using this personal information, content providers can customize their offerings even further
Free content	Included in basic portal services such as Palm.NET	Moviefone; Starbucks Coffee Shop. The revenue gain from providing the mobile device capability has to outweigh the cost of doing so
Content licence fee	Commercial database companies that give limited 'rights-to-redistribute' their content to organizations or portals	Thompson Financial; MapQuest
Value-added pricing	Pricing based on speed of connection or location of user	Streaming content – video, audio, MMS location-based content

regular 'wired' terminals, which require you to be nearby a phone jack and electrical outlet in order to operate. As a result, this has caused many people to find alternative ways to process transactions while they are 'on the road'.

Mobile phones and PDAs have made significant improvements and have added features, one of which is wireless transaction processing. This is the ability to process credit card and debit card transactions wirelessly within seconds at tradeshows, business seminars, house calls, etc.

Before m-commerce solutions became available, collecting funds for orders done 'on the road' required people to pay by cash or cheque, or to write down their credit card information so the transaction could be processed later back at your office. Cash and cheques can get lost, and credit card information, if not put in a secure place, can get into the wrong hands between the information being taken down and the card being charged. M-commerce solutions have taken a lot of the inconvenience out of doing business 'on the run'.

Listed below are the different types of devices with which transactions can be made:

1 *Mobile phone wireless credit card processing.* Wireless processing via your mobile phone is probably one of more cost-effective ways to process cards on the road.
2 *Virtual terminals.* You can do this on a laptop computer that's able to connect to the Internet on a fixed line or on Wi-Fi, then you can process credit card orders securely over any Internet web browser. A virtual terminal is almost always coupled with the purchase of a real-time Internet processing solution. The virtual terminal solution is good because there is no software to install and no long-term, binding leases.
3 *IVR terminals.* Interactive Voice Response terminals provide a relatively new method of being able to process credit cards, cheque cards and cheques via any touch-tone or wireless cell phone. The IVR method greatly reduces chargebacks and fraudulent orders.
4 *PDA and card reader.* This is a PDA wireless processing solution that can be hooked to a card reader so you can obtain the lowest rates possible for your face-to-face transactions.
5 *BlackBerry two-way pager with magnetic card reader.* This allows you wirelessly to process credit and debit cards on the go, and ensures you get the lowest processing rates possible. It greatly decreases the chances of fraud and chargebacks.
6 *Wireless, portable POS swipe terminal.* This is becoming the more advanced area of development, with embedded printers. You can expect to pay a lot for these terminals.

Concerns about e-commerce

Mobile fraud

Mobile fraud is an increasing worry. Fraudsters can literally pluck sensitive information out of the air. The issues are the same as for the fixed-line Internet – transferring sensitive data safely between you and your bank or retailer. The provision of solutions may be made more difficult by the fact that mobile phones are smaller and have less power than desktop computers. Whilst the operators have developed various proprietary systems to manage the taking of payments, as these systems get more sophisticated it is obvious that they are going to be challenged by tricksters, hackers and fraudsters. As we write this book there are no significant cases to study, but this must only be a matter of time.

Speed and power

WAP, or Wireless Application Protocol, is the current mobile Internet platform. It works on:

- the GSM (Global System for Mobile communications) system
- the GPRS (General Packet Radio System)
- the UMTS (Universal Mobile Telecommunications System).

These three can basically be divided into fast, faster and really speedy – anything else is technical details for mobile phone companies to worry about.

Mobile phone companies are concerned about how to make a profit from all of this. If the operators charge high prices for these services, they may find they have broken one of the first rules of Japanese success – keeping it cheap.

The mobile operators aren't the only ones hoping to profit from mobile commerce. The hardware companies and content providers are also a key part of this relationship. The US and Europe diverge in many ways, in both the content and the gadgets they prefer. In Europe, the mobile phone is the hero, and is starting to be used for more than just making and taking calls. Many turn to it for access to online information. In the US, however, small, hand-held computers like the Palm and BlackBerry are assuming the same role. Given that Europe leads the way on phones and the US has taken the lead on handhelds, which one the consumers favour will have significant economic consequences for the companies making the gadgets and the regions they call home. The stage is being set for a showdown.

GSM is the most widely used digital mobile phone system and the *de facto* wireless telephone standard in Europe. Originally defined as a pan-European open standard for a digital cellular telephone network to support voice, data, text messaging and cross-border roaming, GSM is now one of the world's main 2G digital wireless standards. GSM is present in more than 160 countries and, according to the GSM Association, accounts for approximately 70 per cent of the total digital cellular wireless market. GSM is a time division multiplex (TDM) system implemented on 800, 900, 1800 and 1900 MHz. Almost 67 per cent of the 700 million users of digital mobile phones around the world are using GSM phones. As yet, it is unknown whether people will plump for phones that have extras such as diaries and memo pads built-in, or whether they will go for a Personal Digital Assistant (PDA) such as the Palm computer and add-on a phone-call-making widget. Eventually, it may not just be a popularity contest; it is what the technology lets people do that is as important. In that respect, unusually, the US is a long way ahead when it comes to developing sophisticated information-based services.

Devices like the BlackBerry interactive pager and the wireless services introduced with the Palm VII are at the forefront of this innovation. America leads in location-based services that can work out where you are and send relevant information to you.

In June this year, 1000 million text messages were sent from mobile phones in the UK alone. Such things will be key to making an information economy genuinely useful. Personalization and profiling become increasingly important as time goes on to minimize how much the technology has to second-guess the user.

As yet it is a real pain to configure any of these gadgets to make a phone call or manage e-mail on the move. This would defeat the majority of people happy using a mobile phone or sending text (SMS) messages. 'Most people would be horrified by what technology fans put up with to enjoy the latest devices, gadgets and services,' said Andrew Davis, UK Managing Director of Digital Island, which works on getting information to people no matter where they are or what gadget they are using.

There is no doubt that people are keen to use these information-based services. Trials of a system that sends messages about special offers to shoppers at the Thurrock shopping centre near London have almost caused riots as people race to snap up the bargains. A text message offered a free pair of Reebok trainers to whoever turned up at a new shop with their phone, and the store manager was overwhelmed when over 50 people turned up within 4 minutes. Apparently Reebok wasn't going to make a habit of such giveaways.

Configuration challenge

Using a mobile is a great way to manage your life while on the move. The time we have for ourselves is only going to dwindle, and mobile devices are going to be called on to help us more and more. However, they will have to change radically to do so.

Not so long ago, Palm owned the hand-held computer sector, coming out of nowhere to corner almost 80 per cent of the market. In the US at least, Palm was the latest must-have gadget for technophiles everywhere. However, one day in the summer of 2000, software giant Microsoft launched a new line of software for the hand-held market, called Pocket PC, which was to turn its fortunes around.

The company's initial software for handhelds, called Windows CE, had not been a success. Prior to the release of Pocket PC, Microsoft's hardware partners, including Compaq, Casio and Hewlett Packard, had struggled to dent demand for the Palm-based products. However, with the launch of Pocket PC, Compaq's Ipaq became one of the hottest handhelds on the market. The technology research company IDC now expects Windows CE/Pocket PC to account for over 70 per cent of handhelds shipped this year in Western Europe and the US. In 2000, the software only had a 16 per cent market share. After two failed attempts to upgrade Windows CE, Microsoft was finally able to compete with Palm.

'People joke that it takes Microsoft until version three to get something right. Well, this is version three and we got it right,' commented Ben Waldman, Vice-President of Microsoft, at the time.

Despite Microsoft's inroads, the big prizes in the hand-held market are still there to play for. Analysts see tremendous upside in the convergence of handhelds and mobile phones, as well as applications. The PDA market has been very much a niche market, so the real potential is building that functionality into smart phones.

What is also clear is that people do not want to use cut-down PCs. Windows CE handhelds have not been a success compared to Palm or Psion because of the fact that Microsoft has been trying to squeeze PC applications into a smaller mobile device.

Bluetooth

Technologies like Bluetooth, which uses short-range radio, should make it easier to swap information between devices. Bluetooth was developed to realize wireless connection between various types of equipment (mostly small-size ones). The main aim was to provide a small size, low power consumption and a low cost. Ultimately this is good for short distances, and couples well with both mobile wireless and Wi-Fi, but it is unlikely to achieve an great rethink in the bigger picture.

M-commerce scepticism

Commerce on wireless will be struck dead if the network operators charge an extremely expensive tariff. Unfortunately for these operators, they are desperate to claw back some of the money they paid out for the 3G licences. It is hard to see any immediate revenue potential for mobile commerce unless network operators charge low rates for the services, which will finally determine demand; however, the high cost they paid for the licences might leave them with little alternative. Why did the mobile operators pay hand over fist for the licences – surely they must have been sure of their future revenues?

Low charges drove demand for Japanese operator NTT DoCoMo's i-mode service – the mobile Internet's big success story – but these low charges were offset by higher revenues from voice services. Users who found the name of, for example, a local restaurant on i-mode then used their mobile phone to make a reservation. Extra revenue comes from increased voice usage, billing commission, data service charges and extra data traffic, all leading to more time spent online.

NTT DoCoMo takes an estimated 9 per cent commission from transactions conducted on i-mode, with this surprisingly high charge due in part to the billing system it offers content providers (where goods and services ordered on i-mode can be paid for through your telephone bill).

There are other ways that mobile phone operators can boost income – for example, some Internet service providers charge a performance fee if the advertiser receives a certain amount of downloads or page views. Internet-enabled phones could allow people to access corporate intranets or databases while they are on the move.

The mobile alliance

Alliances between the three groups – mobile phone operators, hardware companies and content providers – could complicate revenue streams further. While some content providers may have signed exclusive agreements with mobile operators, most want their content to be seen by as many eyes as possible so as to boost their advertising revenues. Views are mixed as to whether limiting users' mobile experience by allowing them access to a 'walled garden' of content (and thus securing content providers' revenues) could eventually backfire.

Some argue that providing users with a wide mix of services creates a more desirable product. Others believe that controlling access to content by making it easy to use – the key to AOL, the most widely used Internet service provider in the US – will be more effective in creating 'sticky' users who stay with one provider. The advertising market for the mobile Internet is still in its infancy, and worries that this advertising could prove to be intrusive have slowed down the take-up of this type of advertising. The strength of the brand and the interactivity of the content are also likely to influence content providers' revenue.

With future revenue streams uncertain for mobile phone operators and content providers, hardware companies may gain a march in the first round of the battle for profit. However, all three still have some way to go to convince potential users that there are enough attractive and accessible services available to make the system worth buying.

Chapter 8

Mobile spam

Everyone hates spam, whether it appears in their inbox or on their mobile phone. The main problem with mobile spam is that consumers have to pay for receiving unwanted premium text messages, and some scammers have gone as far as to trick users into making premium rate calls from their phones, or to attempt to change the phone device settings. The growing sophistication of spammers has led to an increased amount of mobile spam. Spammers are now venturing beyond the world of e-mail, and are sending messages to phones that are foiling anti-spam technologies which were developed to combat e-mail spam. The operators are becoming wise to spamming techniques, however, and rules and regulations are gradually being put into place and enforced. This will be covered later in this chapter.

Efforts to combat mobile spam face a number of challenges. Spammers are clever enough to set up their operations overseas, where anti-spam laws do not apply, and it is only recently that anti-spam companies have begun to understand wireless networks well enough to be able to combat mobile spam. According to a recent study published by the University of St Gallen in Switzerland, operators who don't figure out how to fight mobile spam risk losing their customers, as most customers blame their operator when they receive unsolicited text messages.

In the UK code of practice for the self-regulation of new forms of content on mobiles, published 19 January 2004, the main mobile operators in the UK (Vodafone, Orange, T-Mobile, O2, 3, and Virgin) state that:

> All those that deliver advertising or promotion through the medium of a mobile device must abide by all relevant Data Protection legislation, including the Privacy and Electronic Communications (EC Directive) Regulations 2003.

On 11 December 2003, laws to implement the EC Directive on Privacy and Electronic Communications 2002 (the 'Directive') were brought into force in the UK under the Privacy and Electronic Communications (EC Directive) Regulations 2003 (the 'Regulations'). The Directive primarily requires EU member states to introduce new laws regulating the use of:

- unsolicited commercial communications (spamming)
- cookies
- location and traffic data
- publicly available directories.

The Regulations apply to providers of public communications networks and services, including the main operators in the UK, traditional businesses operating their own websites and pure e-commerce players. The laws have still broader application in certain circumstances. Ignoring these laws could lead to an investigation and fines, and in some cases criminal liability, which can be brought to bear on a company's directors as well as the company itself.

The following is a summary of the guidelines that should be considered if you are planning on embarking on a mobile marketing campaign. Although many of the guidelines below are more relevant to Internet and e-mail marketing, as handsets become more advanced and e-mail and web browsing becomes common-place these regulations will apply. Because this information is general in nature, you should not act upon it without specific legal advice based on your particular situation.

Unsolicited commercial communications to individuals

Opt-in requirements

The Regulations prohibit the sending of unsolicited electronic communications, such as e-mail, SMS and MMS, if the recipient has not opted in to receive them. An opt-in is usually arranged by the act of ticking a box or clicking an icon when registering for a mailing list, or following an e-mail request for specific information. One exception is when a pre-existing customer relationship is in place; in this case, a business may send unsolicited electronic communications if the following criteria are fulfilled:

- the sender has the contact details of the recipient following a sale or negotiations for the sale of a product or service to that recipient
- the communication is made regarding the sender's similar products and services only

- the recipient is able to refuse (free of charge) the use of his or her contact details for the purposes of sending such communications; this has to be both at the time of the initial collection of the details and at the time of each subsequent communication (an 'unsubscribe' link in an e-mail for example).

Opting out

The Regulations also allow for an individual to opt out of receiving further unsolicited commercial communications at any time. Senders of unsolicited commercial communications must not disguise their identity and must provide a valid contact address so that users can opt out with no difficulty at all.

Corporate subscribers

The Directive has primarily looked to protect individuals from direct marketing. It also obliges the member states to ensure that the interests of non-individuals, i.e. corporate subscribers, are 'sufficiently protected'. Under the Regulations, an opt-out right is provided for corporate subscribers when the address of the recipient contains any personal data – for example, when an e-mail address begins with an actual name rather than with 'info@' or 'company name@'. Sole traders or non-limited liability partnerships in England, Wales and Northern Ireland are not considered to be 'corporate subscribers' under the Regulations.

Use of cookies

Cookies are small bits of data that are left on a user's computer when he or she visits a website. They allow websites to recognize a visitor and track his or her actions and behaviour over a period of time. Site operators can use cookies to check the effectiveness of site content and to see how traffic flows through their site; cookies can also store personal information about a user, so the user does not have to re-enter each time the site is visited. The Regulations prohibit the use of cookies or similar tracking devices unless the person to whom the cookie is served is provided with clear and comprehensive information about the purposes of the storage of, or access to, the information being collected; and is given the opportunity to refuse the storage of or access to that information. The Regulations do not define how this information has to be provided, but state that the text should be 'sufficiently full and intelligible to enable individuals to gain a clear appreciation of the potential consequences of allowing storage and access to the information collected by the device should they wish to do so'. Website operators can make access to a website conditional on the acceptance of cookies, and when cookies are considered to be 'strictly necessary' in order to operate a service requested by the user, the requirements do not apply.

Location and traffic data

Traffic data

The Regulations restrict the use of traffic data, including data related to routing, duration and time of communications. Operators are now obliged to erase personal details once these are no longer necessary for communication, but for billing they can keep personal data for up to six years. If traffic data are to be used for marketing or value-added services, prior consent needs to be obtained from the user.

Location data

Location data allow for the tracking of a user's location geographically. These data can only be processed and used when a user can't be identified or where it is necessary for the provision of a value-added service, such as location-relevant SMS or MMS information. Prior consent is needed before location data can be obtained, and the user must be informed of the type and purpose of the data, and for how long it is going to be held. Consent can be reversed at any time. If the data are going to be sent to a third party, then the user must be informed of this as well.

International marketing

Within the EU, a company's use of personal data will usually be judged and governed by the laws of the country in which the company is based. However, companies should bear in mind that each of the EU member states was allowed to decide whether or not the rights given to individuals should also be extended to corporate subscribers, and some countries have done this to a greater extent than has the UK. In Spain, for example, the same rights have been granted to legal entities as to individuals. If a company from outside the EU targets a citizen of an EU state, that company should be aware that it may be subject to the laws of the relevant state. Legislation and penalties vary between states, so a business embarking on a Europe-wide marketing campaign should look into how the laws are interpreted in the states they are targeting.

Links to the UK's Regulations and other relevant information are set out on the Department of Trade & Industry's website (http://www.dti.gov.uk/industries/ ecommunications/).

Current levels of spam in the industry

The Advertising Standards Authority (ASA) provides one of the main benchmarks against which spam can be measured. The ASA governs the appropriateness of the content of adverts, and though it cannot give a fair representation of mobile spam it can give us an idea of the number of complaints received. It shows that 393 SMS ad complaints were received in 2003, which is a leap up from 65 the previous year. In 2003, SMS was at the bottom of a top-ten list of complained-about media. Network operators do not publish official spam figures but, compared to other forms of spam, the mobile version is still very limited; it is estimated that in Europe half of all e-mails are spam, and in the USA this number is around 70 per cent. The reason mobile spam is still not widespread is because it costs money to send an SMS, which is a huge barrier to scammers or spammers as they cannot generate the same ROI they would be able to with e-mail. Spam text messages and scamming campaigns still exist, however, and there are many scammers who are making money from sending premium rate text messages to users or getting them to call premium rate numbers.

Premium rate activity

How premium numbers and codes work

The Independent Committee for the Supervision of Standards of Telephone Information Services (ICSTIS) tracks premium rate activity, and guidelines can be read on its website at http://www.icstis.org.uk (see Figure 8.1).

If you receive a text or voice message prompting you to call a 090 landline number, this won't have cost you anything. Any general texts prompting you to subscribe to a premium rate text service do not cost anything; they only tend to cost money if you respond to them.

If you respond to a premium rate scam by telephone, costs are as follows:

Number	Cost
090	Typically £1.50 per minute, sometimes £1.00
0871	10 p per minute, not classed as premium rate
070	The limit for these numbers should be 35 p a minute; they are not classed as premium rate

Regarding text scams, in most cases companies can only bill you when they send you a text. If you are still billed whether you open it or not, it is a premium rate message. These messages always come from four- or five-digit numbers (shortcodes). If you are asked to send a message to a shortcode it will only cost you the normal cost of messaging, but you should be careful that you are not subscribing to a premium rate service (i.e. where you receive premium rate texts back). This is particularly the case in the ring-tone market, where users are subscribed automatically to services they text in for after seeing adverts in magazines or the television. Every text the company then sends back to the user will be charged at £1.50, and this can really add up. It is important always to check the small print when responding to one of these adverts.

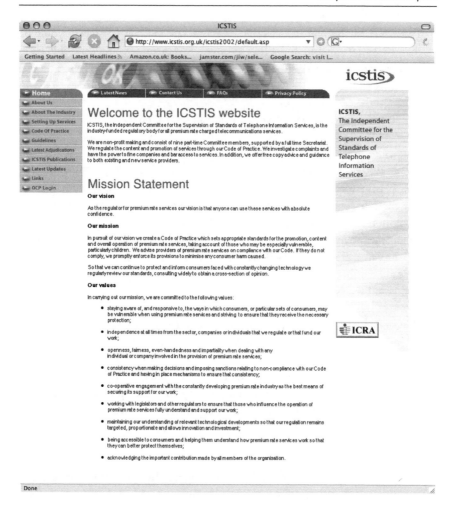

Figure 8.1 *The ICSTIS website (http://www.icstis.org.uk/) – reproduced with permission*

Example scams

Usually the way to avoid premium rate scams is to not reply to anything you haven't asked for; if it is appearing to offer something of value for seemingly nothing, then you should definitely not respond. To give you an idea of the types of scams operating in the UK at the moment, the following are the most common.

1 You'll receive a text asking you to call a premium rate number from a landline to claim a prize. It might look like this:

> Urgent prize claim!! Call 0908123456 from a landline, your complimentary holiday to Spain or £2000 cash is waiting collection

This is a classic prompt to call a 090 premium rate number, for which you'll be charged £1.50 a minute for at least 10 minutes. Any prize you receive will be in the form of vouchers or timeshares.

2 You'll receive a text message saying:

> You have one new MVN voice-mail, call 08718766766 to hear it

The name MVN doesn't mean anything and there is no voice-mail; if you phone the number (which is not premium rate) you'll get put through to a person (or a machine) who will tell you that you have won a prize that must be claimed by phoning a 090 number. The use of a 'first stage' promotion is designed to lull users into a false sense of security, leading to them calling the premium rate number. Other variations on this message prompt you to call a freephone 0800 number for 'customer services' – clearly very misleading.

3 You could receive a text saying:

> Someone you know is trying to contact you through our dating service,
> to see who it is call 09087654567 from a landline

The simple fact is that you are not being contacted by anyone you know; all you will be doing is spending plenty on the premium rate call. Another variation on this theme will ask you to text back rather than call, and any texts you receive from the 'dating service' will then cost you £1.50 each.

The mobile sector has recently been dogged by problems surrounding ambiguous opt-out clauses contained in contracts for services for which they sign up. When consumers try to opt out from a service, they find that they will have to ring a premium rate number for a long period of time, or send a number of text messages. In 2004, ICSTIS fined six companies £500 000 for sending out SMS spam similar to that described above.

Combating unsolicited text messages

The 'Stop' command

There is now a universal command to stop services from legitimate companies, and that is to text the words 'Stop all' or, if this doesn't work, the word 'Stop' to the number from which you received the message. Most companies will remove you from their mailing list if you do this, as many are not keen to attract the attention of ICSTIS.

Checking premium rate numbers

ICSTIS has developed an online service to allow you to check out any premium rate phone or text numbers (http://www.icstis.org.uk/icstis2002/PhoneNumber-Lookup/AskPhoneNumber.asp).

Grumbletext

Another service that has been launched to try to combat unsolicited text messages is Grumbletext, at http://www.grumbletext.co.uk/ (Figure 8.2).

This is a UK consumer complaints and action site. Grumbletext also has a special section called SOS Premium Rate, which has been set up to fight premium rate scams. Scamming companies are reported on the site, and there are lively discussions in the forums on premium rate services.

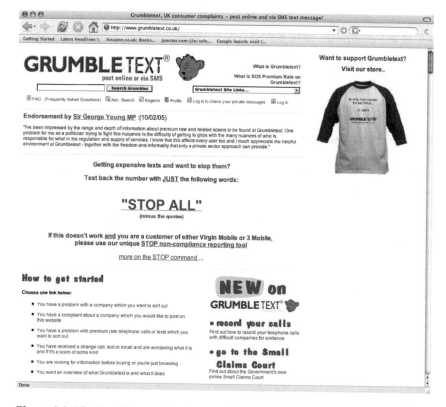

Figure 8.2 *The Grumbletext website (www.grumbletext.co.uk) – reproduced with permission*

For more information regarding the regulation of premium rate services, look at Appendix 2 of the ICSTIS Guidelines for Premium Rate SMS.

ICSTIS Guideline No. 20, Premium Rate SMS (Version 4: March 2005)

Introduction

ICSTIS Guidelines are intended to advise the premium rate services industry on how the Committee interprets or applies provisions in the Tenth Edition of the ICSTIS Code of Practice. Service providers seeking clarity about the application of any Code provision to a particular service are strongly advised to contact the Secretariat before starting to operate the service.

A current list of all of the latest versions of ICSTIS Guidelines appears on the ICSTIS website. Copies of Guidelines are available, free of charge, from the Secretariat.

What are premium rate SMS?

Short Message Services (SMS) enable the transmission of alphanumeric messages between mobile subscribers and external systems such as electronic mail, paging and voice-mail systems.

Scope of this Guideline

This Guideline covers both reverse-billed SMS and SMS where the premium rate charge is applied when the consumer *sends* a text message (SMS mobile origination services), as well as any promotions for either type of service.

Reverse-billed premium rate SMS deliver content to mobile telephone handsets for a charge. Consumers typically subscribe to a service and are then charged a premium for the messages they receive. At present, charges normally range from 10p to £1.50 per message received. However, each mobile network operator determines the exact tariffs applicable.

This Guideline must be read in conjunction with Guideline 17, which deals with unsolicited promotions.

What constitutes a service?

The interpretation of what constitutes a service is largely dependent on what is promised to the consumer in the advertising or marketing material.

For example, if consumers are informed that they will receive a premium rate SMS every day for five days, with each premium rate SMS charged at £x, then the Committee considers the duration of the service to be for the five-day period.

Subscription services are those where a sign-on process initiates a recurring premium rate service. These would include all services billed by a mobile payment mechanism even where the service may be received on a different platform – for example, where a consumer signs up to a service which is paid for by premium rate text messages but is accessed via e-mail.

A single payment for a single product or service constitutes a single service – not a subscription service.

Responsibility for services

Paragraph 3.1 of the Code of Practice states that:

> Service providers are responsible for ensuring that the content and promotion of all of their premium rate services (whether produced by themselves or by their information providers) comply with all relevant provisions of this Code.

The definition of a service provider is contained within Paragraph 1.1.3 of the Code of Practice, which states that:

> A 'service provider' is any person engaged in the provision of premium rate services who contracts with, or enters into arrangements with, a network operator for facilities enabling the provision of premium rate services or who contracts or enters into arrangements with any person who does not fall within section 120(9) of the Act [Communications Act 2003] who has himself contracted with or entered into arrangements with a network operator for such facilities . . .

In the case of premium rate SMS the definition is still applicable, and the service provider is the company that contracts directly with the mobile network(s) regardless of who the content provider may be. This is the company that ICSTIS will turn to and hold responsible for breaches of the Code of Practice. ICSTIS recognizes that breaches can occur as a result of actions taken by third parties (information providers) with whom the service provider may have contracted. In raising any breaches with the service provider, ICSTIS will take all relevant factors into account during the adjudication.

Misleading promotional material

Paragraph 4.3.1 of the Code of Practice states that:

> Services and promotional material must not:
>
> a mislead, or be likely to mislead, by inaccuracy, ambiguity, exaggeration, omission or otherwise,
>
> b be such as to seek to take unfair advantage of any characteristic or circumstance which may make consumers vulnerable.

The Committee is likely to find a breach of the above paragraph of the Code of Practice if a service provider does not adhere to the following guidance:

- Clarity of what the service is. It should be clear to the customer at the outset what a service is and its likely duration. For example, we have had several cases where consumers have not clearly been told that they are entering into a subscription service. Such services and their advertising material have been found to be in breach of the above Code provision. Service providers are encouraged to provide consumers with a free instructional text message regarding what they have signed up to and the frequency with which they will receive premium rate text messages.
- Clarity of instructional information. Service providers are advised to ensure that all promotional material, whether through print media, the Internet, television or transmitted via text message, contains adequate instructions on how the premium rate SMS works.

Where service providers have failed to do this, ICSTIS has found them to be in breach of paragraph 4.3.1(a) ('misleading'). For example, we have adjudicated on several cases where the service provider has been found to be in breach of the ICSTIS Code of Practice, as consumers had not been made aware clearly, or at all, that they were entering a subscription service.

Unsubscribing from services

Service providers should be able to provide unsubscription information in the form of a text message to consumers either before or as soon as reasonably possible after they have subscribed to the service. An opt-out 'request' is considered to be an instructional message, and accordingly should be free.

The unsubscription process should require no more than one text message to take effect. Any messages sent to the consumer confirming exit from the service should be free.

CSTIS has upheld a breach of paragraph 4.3.1(b) ('vulnerability') in cases where consumers have been unable to unsubscribe – for example, due to an over-complicated or convoluted procedure aimed at delaying or preventing someone from opting out of the service.

Universal command to stop services

ICSTIS is aware that the mobile networks have recently amended their contracts with their service providers stating that consumers must be able to exit services when they send the word 'STOP'. ICSTIS has always believed that consumers should be able to exit services whenever they choose.

To this end, the Committee would expect the following to be adopted as for the 'universal command' to stop services:

- The word 'STOP'
- The word 'STOP' can be followed by the service name – for example, 'chat'
- The word 'STOP' with only one space or character between that and the service name.

The command must also not be case sensitive.

Pricing information

Paragraph 4.4.1 of the Code of Practice states that:

> The service provider must state clearly in all promotional material the likely charge for calls to each service. Prices must be noted in the form of a numerical price per minute, or the total maximum cost to the consumer of the complete message or service, both of which must be inclusive of VAT. When applicable, promotional material must make clear that calls from some networks may cost more than the likely charge shown.

Paragraph 4.4.1 of the Code of Practice applies to premium rate SMS in so far as the service provider must clearly state in all promotional material the likely charge for receiving or sending a premium rate text message.

In accordance with paragraph 4.4.2 of the Code of Practice, the pricing information must be legible, prominent, horizontal, and presented in a way that does not require close examination.

The Committee would view it as best practice to state the cost to the consumer of sending a text message to initiate or take part in a reverse-billed premium rate SMS.

The Committee expects the cost of sending non-premium rate text messages to be factored into the total cost by stating, for example, that 'standard operator rates apply for SMS messages sent' or 'call costs range from x pence to y pence per message depending on network'.

Maximum call costs

For all services, the Committee would like to remind service providers that, depending on the service type and the target audience (for example, children), the standard and specific provisions of the ICSTIS Code of Practice will apply. For example, adult services must cost more than £20 and must terminate by forced release. Equally, services specifically targeted at children must terminate after the £3 spend limit has been reached.

Pay-for-product services, which include ring tones, logo, wallpaper and games services (as stated in Guideline 12) must not cost more than £20 in total unless permission to charge otherwise is specifically granted by ICSTIS.

All non-live sexual entertainment services must not cost more than £20 in total (as stated in Paragraph 6.7.7 of the Code).

Instructional messages

Instructional messages are messages that welcome, explain or provide general or specific information about a premium rate SMS service to consumers but are not a substantive part of the service being promoted.

The Committee would not expect the consumer to be charged for pricing information or other instructional messages. Non-exhaustive examples of such messages include an SMS sent:

- confirming that a consumer has entered into a subscription service at £X.x per text, and the duration of the service
- confirming the age of a consumer
- confirming the exit of a consumer from a service
- explaining how a service works, but which does not contain any 'content' or form a substantive part of the service itself.

Address information

Paragraph 4.5 of the Code of Practice states that:

> For any promotion the identity and contact details of either the service provider or information provider, where not otherwise obvious,

must be clearly stated so that customers can contact them directly. The identity means the name of the company, partnership or sole trader and the contact details must consist of one of the following:

a   a full postal address including postcode, or
b   a PO Box number including postcode (PO Box numbers cannot be used in the case of employment, employment information and business opportunity services), or
c   a telephone helpline number (to be charged at no more than UK national rate).

The above information is mandatory for promotions for premium rate SMS, regardless of whether the promotion is advertised through print media, the Internet or television, or by text message.

Data protection

All premium rate SMS service providers should ensure that they process any personal data and mobile phone numbers in accordance with the requirements of the Data Protection Act 1998 and the Telecommunications (Data Protection and Privacy) Regulations 1999, and any other relevant legislation. Further information on these requirements can be obtained from the Office of the Information Commissioner and the website www.dataprotection.gov.uk. In particular, service providers must ensure compliance with paragraph 3.4.3 of the Code of Practice, which states that:

> Services which involve the collection of personal information, such as names, addresses and telephone numbers (which includes the collection of Calling Line Identification (CLI) or caller display information), must make clear to callers the purpose for which the information is required. The service must also identify the data controller (if different from the service provider or information provider) and any different use to which the personal information might be put, and give the caller an opportunity to prevent such usage.

The service provider should store all text messages sent and received by consumers for a period of at least three months.

Requirements for prior permission

Most premium rate services do not require permission from ICSTIS before they can operate, but there are some types of service that require assessment by the

Committee prior to operation, including text chat and dating services, and pay-for-product services.

Text chat and dating services

Under paragraph 3.3.1 of the ICSTIS Code of Practice, the following types of reverse-billed premium rate SMS currently require prior permission from ICSTIS before they can operate:

- services offering 'text chat' services (a text chat service is one that involves an exchange of conversational messages whether it be with a monitor, other consumers or using artificial intelligence to generate responses)
- all SMS contact and dating services.

Please note that services offering 'text chat' services and all SMS contact and dating services that cost 10 p per text or less are excluded from requiring prior permission.

Typical examples of specific conditions that the Committee may impose on such services include the following:

1 *Call cost warning/forced release.* Here, after the consumer had spent £10 he or she would have to be informed of the cost per text message and asked to provide a positive response confirming his or her wish to continue participating in the service. If there were no response from the consumer, the Committee would require the consumer's connection to the service to be terminated.

2 *Pricing requirements.* Here, the Committee might require that the consumer not be charged for receiving the pricing notification or other instructional messages.

3 *Age confirmation.* For 'text chat' services of an adult nature (i.e. sexual entertainment), service providers should ensure that the consumer is over the age of 18 before starting a service. For 'text chat' services of a non-adult nature (i.e. those that can be used by 16-year-olds and above), service providers should ensure that the consumer is over the age of 16 before starting a service. The Committee might require service providers to request either the consumer's date of birth in the form of dd/mm/yy (or a variation thereof) to ensure that the consumer is old enough to take part in the service, or that the consumer should send a text stating his or her age either in numbers or in words. Some niche text chat services (such as a cricket chat service or a service unlikely to lead into general chat topics) may be exempt from having the age check requirements, subject to consideration by the Committee.

4 *Group chat text services.* The Committee may require that consumers must be informed, before they enter the service, of the minimum number of messages (depending on the number of people in the group) they will receive. If there is

a dating element to the 'text chat' service, the Committee may require the imposition of the following conditions: that service providers must warn callers of the risks involved when telephone numbers are given out to other individuals and give clear advice on sensible precautions to take when meeting people through such services; and that service providers should ensure that publicly available elements of the service do not contain telephone numbers, addresses or any other means of direct contact.

5 *Text chat and the youth market.* The Committee has recognized that, for text chat services, there exists a three-tier marketplace: children's services (under-16s); youth services (16–17-year-olds); and adult services (over-18s). Specific conditions are likely to exclude text chat services from being targeted to children (under-16s). However, the Committee is likely to permit non-adult (non-sexual entertainment) text chat services to be offered to the 16–17 age group on the proviso that the advertising of such services occurs in publications where the target readership is not below 16 years of age. With respect to other advertising media, equivalent measures should be taken; for example, such services should not be advertised on television at times when young children may be watching.

Pay-for-product services

Under paragraph 6.6.2, pay-for-product services likely to cost more than £20 require prior permission from ICSTIS before they can operate. Typical examples of specific conditions that the Committee may impose on such services may include the following.

1 *Promotional material.* Promotional material for subscription services must clearly indicate that the service is subscription based. Such information should be prominent and highly visible to readers. Subscription services terms of use (e.g. whole cost pricing, opt-out) information should be clearly visible. Wherever 'Stop' instructions are displayed, the information provided must advertise the generic STOP command, and additionally service-specific stop commands – for example, 'stop polytones' may also be advertised.

2 *Subscription initiation.* Initial subscription messages must contain the following information: name of service; confirmation that the service is subscription based; the billing period (i.e. per day, per week or per month); how much the user is charged for that billing period; how to leave the service (including the generic stop command); and service operator contact details. These points should be in the first message(s) sent to the customer, and must before any promotional content is provided. They must be in a free-to-receive message(s). The initiation of any form of subscription service should result in the initial subscription message being sent to the handset.

3 *Subscription reminders*. Once a month, the following information shall be sent to subscribers: name of service; that the service is subscription based; what the billing period is (i.e. per day, per week or per month); how much the user is charged for that billing period; and service operator contact details. Subscription service users must also be sent a reminder of the 'Stop' command; the frequency is determined by the cost of the service, and service providers must also send a 'Stop' command reminder every time the total spend reaches £20 since the last 'Stop' command reminder. If the service is designed to cost less than £20 per month, the service provider must send the 'Stop' command reminder every month instead of when £20 has been spent.

4 *Subscription termination*. After a user has sent a 'Stop' command to a service, the service operator should not submit any further billed messages for the relevant service. Users must be free to leave a service at any time and service providers must do nothing to indicate otherwise unless specific permission to do so has been granted.

How to contact ICSTIS

ICSTIS, Clove Building, 4 Maguire Street, London SE1 2NQ.

Tel: 020 7940 7474
Fax: 020 7940 7456
Free helpline: 0800 500 212
London Press Office: 020 7940 7408
E-mail: secretariat@icstis.org.uk
Website: www.icstis.org.uk

Chapter 9

Measuring results

Technologies such as Wireless Application Protocol (WAP) and i-mode are enabling companies to design miniature Internet sites, specially created for mobile phones with smaller displays and 'thin' connections. The mobile Internet or wireless Internet is still in its infancy, and its impact could be far greater than that of the PC-based version.

Wapper and targeted advertising

Advertiser-supported wireless sites use one of several business models in this emerging medium. Currently, there are three major types of advertiser-supported sites:

1 Sponsored content sites
2 Sponsored search agents and directories
3 Entry portal sites like Vodafone Live! (these sites in most instance are owned by the network operator).

At present, these three classes of sites are split at about 20 per cent, 20 per cent and 60 per cent, respectively, in terms of advertising revenue.

Advertising is expected to be an increasingly significant source of revenues in this new medium. Sponsored content is attractive because it is well suited to the wireless environment, yet retains important parallels to existing media in the physical world. Many wireless managers are beginning to place more importance on advertising revenue streams as a source of profitability for online content.

Against this backdrop, firms are trying to understand what makes wireless advertising successful. As advertisers and marketers debate the best ways to measure and track visits and usage on commercial wireless sites, most firms remain largely in the dark about how many customers exist online for their offerings. Because the industry currently lacks standards regarding what to measure and how to measure it, the wireless Internet is having difficulty being accepted as an advertising medium and there is no assurance that firms will be successful in generating significant revenues from advertising in the future. Ultimately, the lack of standardization will limit the long-term viability of the advertising model.

The complexity of the medium in general hinders the standardization process. First, there are no established principles for measuring traffic on commercial wireless sites that seek to generate revenues from advertising sponsorship. Second, there is no standard way of measuring consumer response to advertisements. Third, there are no standards for optimal media pricing models.

The perception persists that wireless-based advertising efforts are not and may never be serious. In part this may be because traditional advertising spending easily dwarfs current wireless advertising efforts. For example, the price of a single 30-second television spot on prime-time's top show is currently $750 000. Wireless advertising expenditures represent a medium in its infancy, with a spend of only $30 000.

Yet the scepticism can more importantly be traced to the fact that few have specified conclusively just how advertising on wireless can and should further a firm's strategic marketing objectives. Clearly, standardizing the wireless measurement process is a critical first step on the path toward the successful commercial development of the wireless Internet.

The objectives of this chapter are:

- To review practices for advertising measurement in traditional media
- To examine current practice for advertising measurement on wireless, drawing comparisons to methodologies used in traditional media research
- To propose a methodology for wireless advertising measurement
- To offer recommendations for wireless advertising research.

In addition to proposing a set of 'basic elements' and 'exposure data' that define the consideration set of possible measures, we also introduce a set of interactivity and time metrics that we believe must be included in any complete program for wireless measurement. We look at what data is required in order to calculate a particular metric and remain aware of the link between wireless metrics and media pricing models. We would welcome adoption by the marketplace of specific metrics for judging the effectiveness of advertising.

Advertising measurement terminology

We have always proposed to our clients that if there is terminology from traditional media that it is appropriate to use in the context of wireless-based advertising, then it should be used to avoid confusion and ease the adoption of standards. We begin by providing a glossary of the standard definitions for key measures in print and broadcast. These measures are used in most media audience evaluations and for current comparisons across mass media planning.

- *Gross impressions/impressions*. The gross sum of all media exposures, which is made up of numbers of people or homes. This does not take into account duplication.
- *Reach*. The number of (unduplicated) people or households that will be exposed to an advertising campaign at least once over a specified period of time.
- *Effective reach*. The number of people who are exposed to an ad at the 'effective frequency'.
- *Frequency*. The number of times that an individual is exposed to a particular advertising message in a given period of time.
- *Effective frequency*. The number of exposures needed for an ad to become 'effective'. In mass media models, effective frequency stipulates the amount of exposure that is necessary before it is effective, and is used interchangeably with effective exposures. Research indicates that less than three exposures will not allow adequate recall.
- *CPM*. Cost per thousand impressions. This is the cost per 1000 people delivered by a medium or media schedule.
- *Duplication*. The number or percentage of people who see an advertisement or campaign in two or more situations.
- *Gross rating points*. GRP provide a measure of scheduling impact calculated on a weekly or monthly basis. GRP for mass media can be calculated as multiplying the reach by frequency. This is expressed as a percentage of prospects in the target market exposed to television and/or magazine vehicles carrying the ad.
- *Share*. 'Share of audience' is the percentage of users on a particular page or site. 'Share of market' is the percentage of advertising impressions generated by all brands in a category accounted for by a particular brand, but often also refers to share of media spending.
- *Ratings*. The percentage of a given population group consuming a medium at a particular moment. This is generally used for broadcast media, but can be used for any medium. One rating point equals 1 per cent.

- *Composition.* The mixture of audience characteristics found in the audience for a medium or campaign. It also refers to the percentage of some mediums' total audience made up of the target segment.
- *Cost per inquiry.* This is the cost to generate an inquiry in direct-response advertising, and is calculated by the total cost of the direct-response advertising divided by the number of inquiries it generates.

Current advertising on the wireless Internet

Banner ads and target ads are a primal form of advertising, but for wireless-based advertising this may ultimately be the most effective. We noted early on that the small screen size of a mobile phone meant that it was hard to standardize a graphic format; therefore we invented the 'wapper'. This is a banner ad that might simply be text emboldened in the body copy or it might be a graphic. In either instance, the wapper points out to promotional content 'targeted ad'.

Thus two primary forms of wireless-based advertising exist: wapper and target ads. Active exposure of target ads is under the consumer's control; passive ad exposure to wapper is under the marketer's control. This distinction has important implications for the measurement process.

A wapper ad is a small, typically rectangular, graphic image in a variety of sizes which is linked to a target ad. Wappers typically provide little information other than the identification of the sponsor, and serve as an invitation for the visitor to click on the graphics to learn more. Wappers are a form of passive advertising exposure, in that the consumer does not consciously decide to view the ad. Rather, the wapper is presented as an outcome of accessing a particular wireless content page, or of entering a series of key words into a search engine. Wappers placed on homepages of general-interest sites or on the entry page of a search engine would have lower click rates than ads that are consistent with the content of narrowly targeted wireless sites, or a wapper presented by a search engine in response to specific keywords (e.g. ads for Java games presented every time a visitor searches for 'Games' or for 'Java'). Figure 9.1 is an example of just such a targeted ad that users find from a wapper.

Paid links are a different form of passive advertising, and may be most simply viewed as a text version of a banner ad. Paid links are often incorporated in directories, which may contain large numbers of such paid links.

Active ad exposure is under the consumer's control; passive ad exposure is under the marketer's control. The distinction between passive and active advertisements

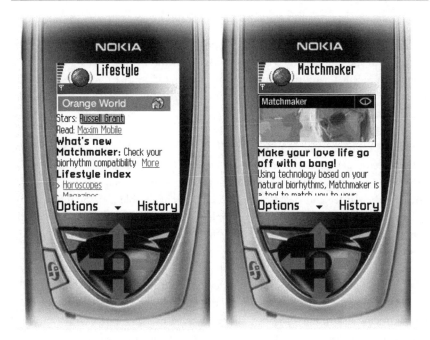

Figure 9.1 *A WAP portal link from Orange world to MatchMaker – reproduced with permission*

implies a crucial difference between banner and target ads. The concept of an active advertisement is a feature that differentiates wireless or web advertising from advertising in traditional media.

Most of the focus in wireless advertising measurement has been on banner advertisements. This is probably because their passive nature means wappers have many more parallels with traditional media planning than do active ads. The factors that affect selection in print media should also impact on the selection of wappers. These factors are closely tied to the 'creative' function in advertising, and include size, position, directionality, motion, colour, intensity, contrast and novelty, all of which we would expect to be useful for predicting the likelihood that a visitor will click on a wapper.

Pricing models

Currently, exposure models, based on CPM or flat fees applied to site exposure or banner ad exposure, are the dominant approach to wireless media pricing. Fees based on actual click-throughs are also in use, where the advertiser pays for actual clicks on a banner ad that leads to the advertiser's target ad.

Flat fee pricing consists of a fixed price for a given period of time, and flat fees are the most common model in the current wireless advertising business. Flat fee pricing can be implemented either with or without traffic guarantees. At a minimum, accurate information regarding site traffic must be made available to the advertiser so that the advertiser can evaluate the decision to go with the flat fee approach.

Assuming accurate traffic information, flat fee prices can be readily converted into a CPM (cost per thousand exposures) model. CPM can also be enhanced by providing 'guarantees' of the number of impressions in a given period of time. We consider the flat fee and CPM models to be interchangeable if traffic information, specifying the number of visitors to a wireless site, is available. If traffic information is not available, then flat fee pricing can still be used, although it is then impossible to evaluate.

The advertiser-supported business model has initially gravitated toward CPM as the appropriate unit of measure. In this model, the belief is that exposure-based pricing takes into account different advertisers' response functions and represents a rational way to price advertising on the wireless. However, in fact impression/exposure models go only part of the way because wireless is different from traditional broadcast media. The wireless Internet is based on a one-to-one communication model and traditional media are based on a one-to-many communication model. The CPM approach places too much emphasis on the wapper and essentially no emphasis on the target ad — which is the 'real' marketing communication that the advertiser wishes the visitor to see and interact with. In addition to exposure metrics, we therefore also need inter-activity metrics.

CPM and flat fee models do nothing more than simply count the number of visitors exposed to a particular banner advertisement on a site. As consumer behaviour on the wireless Internet depends on a whole host of measurable factors, including the type of site and the consumer's motivation for visiting it, a simple count of visits is not sufficient to demonstrate value to the advertiser of their advertising expenditures. It is meaningless to compare directly the number of visitors exposed to wappers across pages. The CPM model is of larger numbers being bigger winners because the one-to-many model seeks a mass audience for its message. The danger of relying solely on exposure models means that interactive managers will be driven to scale their sites to larger, mass audiences with more homogeneous tastes in order to attract more advertising revenue. This is in contrast to solving the more difficult problem of how to measure interactivity and price advertising according to the value of a consumer's interactive visit to the advertiser through his or her spend.

Ad pricing based on click-through

This is an attempt to develop a more accountable way of charging for wireless advertising. The payment for a banner ad is based on the number of times a visitor actually clicks on it. A relatively small proportion of those exposed to a banner ad actually click on the banner. Click-through rates drop off after the first exposure, falling to 2 per cent for the second and third exposures, and 1 per cent or less at four exposures. Payment based on click-through guarantees that the visitor was not only exposed to the banner ad, but also actively decided to click on the banner and become exposed to the target ad. Click-through payment can be viewed as payment for target ad exposures.

The click-through is at least partially a function of the 'creative' and not under the publisher's control. On the other hand, as we have seen, applying only traditional media exposure models to the wireless Internet does not take into account its unique, interactive nature. Additionally, the Internet, whether mobile or landline based, is the first commercial medium in which it is actually possible to measure consumer response, rather than just assuming it.

Interactivity

While payment based on click-through guarantees exposure to target ads, it does not guarantee that the visitor liked the ad, or even spent any substantial time viewing it. A measure can be applied to the visitor's interaction with the target ad, and such an interactivity metric might be based on the time spent viewing the ad, the depth or number of pages of the target ad accessed, or the number of repeat visits to the target ad. In an ideal world you should pay not for exposures or click-through, but only for activity/traffic at your site generated from this advertising. This raises controversy surrounding the best wireless media pricing models, with wireless publishers arguing that the problem with activity-based measures like click-through or interactivity is that the wireless publisher cannot be held responsible for the activity related to an advertisement. After all, in print you get charged for ads whether or not they lead to sales. In the long run, the solution will probably be found by accepting the reality that the medium and the advertisement interact, and all parties share responsibility for outcomes.

Outcome-based approach to pricing

The metrics discussed so far relate to early stages of the purchase process. The wapper affects the consumer's awareness, and interaction with the target ad affects the consumer's comprehension and understanding. These initial stages are the marketing objectives of attitude change, purchase intention and, ultimately, purchase.

An outcome-based approach to pricing wireless advertising begins by specifying exactly what the marketer would like the target ad to do. Examples of typical outcomes include motivating the consumer to provide information about him- or herself, influencing attitudes, or leading the consumer to purchase. Whatever the marketing objective, the wireless Internet provides a vehicle for integrated marketing campaigns that allows the marketer to track and measure the advertisement's effectiveness. The need to set in place tools to measure and identify visitors and their interaction is paramount. Unless you have this data, the measurement of outcome remains elusive.

Standards and auditing

Most organizations involved in web standards have signalled their intent to set measurement standards for wireless advertising. The point of such standards is to facilitate the measurement process, and to identify what should be measured and how. Many things will affect a universal standards setting process, including whether trust in the auditing function requires an independent third party in the measurement process, and how to protect consumer privacy in the face of extensive 'clickstream' data collection efforts. The auditing process involves the objective evaluation of transaction counts by an independent agency. The purpose of the audit is to produce validated data that permit advertisers to compare wireless sites in the context of the media buy. A 'trusted' third party is sought to avoid any potential or actual conflicts of interest. In the wireless medium, the auditing function is served by both traditional media auditors and firms that engage in the measurement process. Third-party audits are necessary for potential advertisers to trust traffic claims of wireless sites, but that is not always the case. If you have a strong enough brand, no one will come up to you and say that they will not buy space on your site because you haven't had an independent audit. This is different, because a brand name indicates quality. The key issue is therefore advertiser trust.

The need to know and measure

What do people do on the mobile web? Why are they doing it? As most would agree that hits are meaningless as comparative measures of visitor behaviour, wireless sites now tend to report visits. What exactly does a 'visit' mean? Can wireless publishers provide even the most basic descriptive statistics about their sites, including how many unique visitors are coming, how often users visit, where they tend to come from, how long they stay, the average number of pages per visit, the four or five most popular navigation patterns through the site, the most popular pages, the least popular pages, and so on?

To start to know the capability of a site for advertising you really need to:

- define visits to site
- describe consumer behaviour during a visit
- relate visits to interactivity and outcomes/sales.

Such data are critical to demonstrate the viability of the wireless as a commercial medium, and provide mechanisms for tracking usage as well as measuring investment opportunities and business success.

Definitions of hits

When visitors reach a wireless site, their device sends a request to the site's server to begin displaying pages. Each element of a requested page including graphics, text or interactive items is recorded by the site's server log file as a 'hit'.

Hits have been widely criticized as a measure of wireless traffic. While the definitions of hits are quite consistent, the weakness of hits as a valid measure of traffic to a wireless site is quite evident. Since hits include all units of content (images, text, sound files) sent by a wireless server when a particular URL is accessed, hits are inherently non-comparable across wireless sites because some sites might have numerous assets per page whilst others have a text block and one graphic. We believe there is no validity to reporting hits. Other than ignorance of the meaninglessness of hits, the only reason we feel a wireless site would report the number of hits is that this is typically a large and very impressive sounding number. Other definitions include:

- *Clicks*. Clicks are Page Information Requests (PIRs) and successful Page Information Transfers (PITs). PITs provide a true measurement of page deliveries going beyond page requests.
- *Visitors/users*. Visitors or users represent individuals who visit wireless sites. The definitions differ according to how much is known about an individual visitor/user.
- *Visits and sessions*. A visit is commonly defined as a sequence of requests made by one user. Once a visitor stops making requests from a site for a given period of time, called a time-out, the next hit by this visitor is considered to be a new visit. To simplify comparisons, we have always used the Internet rule of a 30-minute time-out to determine the start of a new visit. You can also determine site visits by adding visits from single-user Internet addresses, which can be tracked and identified, to a count of multi-user addresses.

- *Ad views, page views, site visits.* These are exposure measures, and give the number of times an ad banner is downloaded and presumably seen by visitors. If the same ad appears on multiple pages simultaneously, ad views may be understated due to browser caching.
- *Ad clicks/click-through.* These are interactivity measures, and give the number of times users 'click' on an ad banner to request additional information from the advertiser. Typically, users are directed to the advertiser's wireless site. Sometimes referred to as 'click-through rate,' this is the number of ad clicks as a percentage of ad views.
- *Duration time.* This is an interactivity measure, and gives the average time spent by a user on a single wireless page. Users have the ability temporarily to leave a wireless site and then return to the same page via the 'back' button in their browser, so the average time spent on a page will not be 100 per cent accurate. However, for a highly viewed page, the average time on page will be nearly 100 per cent accurate.

Wireless advertising measurement

There are three distinct levels of analysis for wireless advertising measurement:

1 Campaign level
2 Page level
3 Ad level.

The ultimate objective is linking the various measures to consumer outcomes to quantify the value of a visit.

For each level of analysis, you need exposure data and interactivity data. Exposure data are based on the one-to-many communication model underlying traditional media, and indicate that a visitor has been exposed to a wireless site, a wireless page or an advertisement. Interactivity data are based on the one-to-one communication model underlying the wireless Internet, and indicate the extent to which the visitor actively engages with the wireless content or advertisement.

Considering these three levels of analysis, Table 9.1 presents traditional media analogues and examples of currently used exposure data. It summarizes our behavioural exposure and interactivity.

Definitions of metrics

To obtain banner ad exposure, it is necessary to have one of unidentified, session, tracked or identified visitors, plus information concerning whether the visitor was exposed to the wapper or not.

Table 9.1 *Summary metrics for wireless measurement*

	Campaign level	Page level	Ad level
Exposure data	Site exposures	Page exposures	Banner ad exposures
	Site exposure	Page reach	Target ad exposures
	Duplication	Page frequency	Banner ad reach
	Site reach		Target ad reach
	Site frequency		Banner ad reach
			Duplication
			Banner ad frequency
			Target ad frequency
			Banner ad visit
			Frequency
			Target ad visit
			Frequency
Interactivity data	Visit duration time	Page duration time	Banner ad exposures
	Inter-visit duration time		Target ad exposures
	Raw visit depth		Banner ad reach
	Visit depth		Target ad reach
			Banner ad reach
			Duplication
			Banner ad frequency
			Target ad frequency
			Banner ad visit
			Frequency
			Target ad visit
			Frequency

Additional measurement tools

In addition to the measures we have described in this chapter so far, there are additional statistics that could and should be considered in the context of wireless advertising measurement. While we do not discuss these additional measures in this chapter, you should be aware of them. They include:

- cross-site navigation patterns
- behavioural characteristics, demographic and psychographic, of visitors to a wireless site, and to specific pages within a wireless site
- loyalty and repeat visits.

In addition to the behavioural and psychological measures, results-driven data must be developed. As the models most frequently applied to the wireless are based on traditional, mass media models, it makes sense to consider the direct-response paradigm. This is when any direct communication to a consumer or business recipient is intended to generate a response in the form of a direct order, a request for further information and/or a visit to a store or other place of business for purchase of a specific product or service. The concepts of 'direct order', 'lead generation' and 'traffic generation' are immediately and obviously applicable in many traditional media:

- *Direct order* includes all direct-response advertising communications – through any medium – that are specifically designed to solicit and close a sale. All of the information necessary for the prospective buyer to make a decision to purchase and complete the transaction is conveniently provided in the advertisement.
- *Lead generation* includes all direct-response advertising communications – through any medium – that are designed to generate interest in a product or a service, and provide the prospective buyer with a means to request and receive additional information about the product or service.
- *Traffic generation* includes all direct-response advertising communications conducted – through any medium – that are designed to motivate the prospective buyer to visit a store, restaurant or other business establishment to buy an advertised product or service.

It is obvious that definitions and data developed from considering the wireless site as a unique hybrid of direct response and traditional communication media will lead to the optimal set of models for measurement and pricing.

Recommendations

Both exposure and interactivity metrics may make contributions to various stages in the planning model; banner ad reach/frequency/exposure will be related to awareness, while target ad duration time and depth will be related to comprehension. By understanding the influencing mechanisms, we can take action to increase ad click-through rates. Response functions, such as the optimal number of exposures to a banner ad within and across visits, must be determined, and have clear implications for dynamic placement of a wapper based on a visitor's previous history of exposure to the ad.

We are ultimately interested in identifying the exposure and interactivity data that determine advertising prices. Currently, most of the focus seems to be on paying for wappers, which simply deliver exposures to target ads. It is not clear that this is necessarily money well spent. If the marketing objective is to increase consumer comprehension of a firm's product-line offerings, then it would make sense for the advertiser to pay more for visitors who spend a greater amount of time viewing the target ad, and who view more pages of the target ad.

Policy and privacy considerations

Many marketers feel that privacy is a 'commercially valuable benefit', and that protecting consumer privacy is actually consistent with customization to customer needs in the online environment. The specific issues here are what information we are gathering from consumers, whether they know we are gathering it, and what we plan to do with it. There is tension between the marketer's need to know information about individual consumers for the purposes of targeted marketing efforts, and the consumer's right to privacy. We believe the ultimate solution to this conflict is to enter into a full partnership with consumers in which they control ownership of their demographic and behavioural data, and determine how and when these will be used. This solution respects the underlying business model in which consumers can also be providers to the medium, allowing them to remain active participants in the interactive communication process.

We believe that the overriding principle that must guide efforts is the one of 'opt-in', in which the consumer is informed about the privacy consequences of their online behaviour prior to engaging in it. This is in stark contrast to the more common 'opt-out' policy prevalent in the physical world, in which consumers may never know that data is being collected about them and possibly resold to others without their knowledge.

Mobile phone users value their privacy, visiting sites anonymously or by adopting various aliases depending on the circumstances of the content. Users desire complete control over whether a particular wireless site should receive any information on them. While users recognize that marketers require demographic and behavioural data about visits for business purposes, users do not feel that marketers have the right to sell this information to other firms. Wireless users seemed willing to provide demographic information if marketers will tell them what is being collected and how it will be used.

'Disguised wappers' are potentially of ethical concern. Suppose that an advertiser-supported search agent site presents links to an advertiser's wireless site positioned at the top of a list produced by a search request for a set of keywords. In this case, while the requester may believe that a link appears at the beginning of the list because it is the most relevant to his or her keyword request, the top position of the link may be due to sponsor payments. Such practices must be made clear to users of the search agent, as they have the potential to deceive consumers and undermine trust in search tools and seemingly useful community sites.

Strategic considerations

Strategic considerations that need to be addressed when developing advertising measurement include:

- *Target marketing*. Wireless sites must facilitate one-to-one marketing by permitting customization and tailoring of content and user interface. The navigating experience can be tailored to user's preferences or device type, so that different visitors see advertisements most appropriate to their interests. Most current practice in wireless advertising measurement ignores the fact that wireless content and ads can be tailored to segments or groups of respondents. This creates a final click-through message of 'No content is available for this device'.

- *Comparability*. What is the difference between a wireless site that does not incorporate user-driven customization and a wireless site that does incorporate customization? It might be expected that a certain number of ad exposures at a site that targets ads according to user preferences or demographics would be more effective than the equivalent number of exposures at a site that presents a single ad to all visitors.

- *Isolated* v. *coordinated ad placement*. A media plan will typically involve a set of sites, based on a decision that takes into account the cost-effectiveness of placing ads on various sites. However, in these initial states of wireless-based advertising it should be expected that much of the current state-of-the-art of wireless ad placement is based on an isolated rather than a coordinated media buying strategy. Effective wireless measurement needs to recognize that coordinated, rather than isolated, ad placement is more desirable, and that measurement of visitor duplication across wireless sites is fundamental to the final decision. The strategic issue of isolated v. coordinated ad placement relates to the diffusiveness of payment for wireless advertising. On one hand are large sums for ads placed on relatively small numbers of sites viewed by large numbers of visitors, while on the other hand are micropayments for ads placed on large number of sites each viewed by relatively small number of visitors. One example of a similar approach is used by the amazon.com Associates program. In this program, any site can place a link to one of 300 000 books sold by Amazon.com and receive a royalty for all sales that occur as a result of a visitor accessing Amazon.com via that link.

- *Depth* v. *Breadth*. There are two complementary approaches to collecting visitor data for advertising measurement. Server access logs focus on depth, and in theory provide a complete record of all traffic to a given wireless site. However, caching by the user's browser and caching of wireless pages by Internet service causes the server access log to be an incomplete record, and an underestimate of true traffic. Registration, or tracking via cookies, can combine in-depth with breadth of data across multiple wireless sites.

- *Viability of the advertising sponsorship model*. Finally, an important strategic consideration is the long-term viability of the advertising sponsorship model. Advertising sponsorship is by no means the only viable method for supporting commercial wireless sites. While advertising is currently the dominant business model on the web and wireless, online store fronts, subscriptions and micropayments provide alternative business models with considerable potential.

Previously, we observed that CPM and flat fee models do nothing more than count the number of visitors exposed to a particular banner ad at a particular site. We proposed a pricing model based on interactivity metrics. The rationale behind this argument is that the degree to which the visitor interacts with the target ad is a better measure of the value and effectiveness of an ad. We are looking at measuring the revenue spent as a cornerstone of effectiveness.

Ultimately, marketers are interested in outcomes, and the ultimate outcome is purchase.

Chapter 10

Budgeting and planning

Today, companies are focusing on wireless solutions that can deliver a faster ROI and increased productivity at the same time as increasing their marketing reach. Many view mobile wireless technology as a prime tool for increasing employee productivity and reducing costs, giving an immediate positive effect on the bottom line.

Analysts agree that mobile wireless technology spending will continue to increase over the next five years. According to a report by Jupiter Media Metrix, IT managers are budgeting for enterprise wireless deployments. In a recent survey of IT executives, Jupiter found that 27 per cent expect to apportion at least $2 million of their budgets to wireless projects within the next three years. The bursting of the Internet bubble has made management very cautious regarding the digital economy.

Despite the consequences of whether firms seek short-term savings or recognize a longer-term return prospect, mobile wireless initiatives should incorporate machinery that helps to increase efficiencies, reduce uncertainties and focus on the bottom line. In a demanding economy, those wireless strategies that will succeed are those that drive savings in the short term without themselves being short-term. We have listed below considerations to bear in mind when planning a mobile wireless strategy.

1 *Think evolutionary, not revolutionary.* A firm should view wireless not as an entirely new strategy, but as an extension to their existing marketing digital plans. Leveraging the full potential of a firm's marketing strategy significantly decreases the complexities of implementation and management, and will enable enterprises to scale and evolve to meet future needs. By implementing a wireless

solution that leverages existing strategy rather than all-new ones, firms will find that the results are more manageable with fulfilment at lower cost. The focus should be on open planning that builds upon and integrates with existing digital strategy and infrastructures.

2 *Choose integrated solutions that build on current experience.* Ad hoc product implementations, although sometimes easy to put into practice, usually result in long-term management headaches and burdensome support overheads. This can mean prohibitive cost of ownership, and missed market opportunities due to an inflexible services platform. Best-of-breed solutions designed to meet a firm's individual needs will confer greater returns on investment and increased business agility in the short term and beyond only if internal teams of marketers and IT specialists get involved in the process. Such an approach creates a community of experienced individuals who already understand the firm's workings. Once extended strategy is bedded down, the solution becomes scalable and provides optimal functionality and performance, minimizes cost and maximizes return on investment.

3 *Demand open standards.* Open standards enable a firm to select from the best-of-breed solutions without fear of vendor lock-in. By utilizing open standards, an enterprise can 'future-proof' its technology investments and position itself to take maximal advantage of new technologies and business opportunities. These are easily integrated into assorted infrastructures and allow for optimal cost and performance effectiveness.

Initial set-up

Like all marketing programs, the initial set-up is the same. The concept development stage is where we are trying to do a number of things, including producing an initial budget outline. This is the first stage approach:

1 Determine the objectives of the marketing program and target audience.
2 Develop concepts to meet the program objectives.
3 Evaluate the costs of running the campaign against budget. Things to consider include:

- cost of set-up of delivery mechanism (monthly or annual payment)
- cost of running the mechanism considering monthly fees for hire of shortcodes and the usage cost per user or SMS
- building management interface for all data
- resources to support the campaign in the field.

4 Preliminary recommendations on how to extend the program and maximize the budget through promotions, partnerships, public relations and sponsorship.

General guidelines for mobile marketing

All mobile marketing must be carried out in accordance with the countries' legislation and codes of practice (see Appendix C for guidelines and legislation bodies in mobile marketing).

In principle, all mobile marketing must be carried out in a manner that is:

- legal
- decent
- honest
- truthful
- permission-based
- responsible
- responsive
- respectful.

What is considered to be legal and decent can vary dramatically between countries and cultures, so always check locally and build time into your project schedule to do this. There is nothing more disturbing to an individual than getting an indecent SMS.

Build out the budget and projectize all components of the program

This includes:

- carrying out concept research, program naming, program scheduling and routing
- developing on-site web/WAP activities
- deciding on a preliminary design
- making a detailed budget analysis
- developing a plan for each support element (advertising, public relations, promotions, etc.)
- carrying out preliminary testing or prototyping of the campaign.

Decide on your target group

Given the personal nature of mobile marketing, you must take particular care to ensure that all content is appropriate to the relevant target group and in the context of the campaign. A significant percentage of all complaints received in relation to mobile marketing campaigns relate to what is perceived by the complainant as inappropriate content. This is quite damaging to any brand. Before doing anything else, you need to decide what target group the campaign is aimed at and how to ensure that the proposed content/form of the campaign is appropriate for that target group. How offensive or inappropriate it might be considered to be will vary depending on the target group and the context of the campaign. You must take all reasonable steps to ensure, if you are involved in any of the above types of marketing, that such marketing is only sent to an appropriate target group. In particular, you must not send any marketing relating to alcohol, tobacco, gambling services or products, cosmetic surgery or adult products to under-18s. Only send marketing relating to adult products or material to recipients who are 18 or over, who have specifically consented to receive such adult marketing, and who are age verified.

You must also decide how you will find out whether the user is likely to take up the offer, and ensure that all content is clear and is not misleading or deliberately baffling. Finally, you have to ask yourself the question, does it make sense?

The frequency of a campaign

The frequency of a campaign is important from both spamming and cost points of view. When sending mobile marketing communications, you must be sensible in relation to the timing, volume and frequency.

The time of day is important, and you will need a great deal of advice to line up your product with users and their leisure time. In addition, it is not acceptable to send mobile marketing communications aimed at children so that it is received at a time when they might reasonably be expected to be asleep. Do this at your peril: angry parents are a nightmare for customer services, and it just does not make sense to market your company badly.

Using opt-in and soft opt-in

You must only send mobile marketing to people who have agreed in advance to your doing this (i.e. on an opt-in basis). There is an exception to this; you can send mobile marketing to people whose details you have obtained in the course of the sale of a product or service to that person, or in the course of negotiations for the sale of a product or service even if this does not actually result in a sale. You must give them the opportunity to opt out of receiving mobile marketing at the time you first collect their details. However, it is best practice only to use any details obtained on a soft opt-in basis for the purpose of contacting the relevant people to ask them to opt in to receive further mobile marketing communications from you and to delete their details if you have not received an opt-in response from them within 48 hours of having requested this.

Terms and conditions

Where a campaign is being publicized by promotional material, such as a card given out in shops, or posters, then the basic information should include suitable opt-in wording and a means of obtaining access to the full terms and conditions and privacy statement – for example, a website address or a phone number. If you are providing a website address, then it is good practice also to provide a phone number. You must not use premium lines that exceed the national standard rate. Best practice dictates that when providing a phone number, it should be a freephone number where possible.

If you are using a mechanism such as a card given out in shops or on the street, then it is useful to give a code (this can be a codeword or a number) that needs to be texted back to you in order for the customer to enter the promotion. This confirms that each person entering the promotion has seen the information held on the card.

Marketing to children

All mobile marketing to children must be carried out in a responsible and sensitive manner, and be appropriate to the target age group. If you are including games, competitions, prize promotions or prize draws, you will find the 'dos and don'ts' given here very useful.

1 *Collection of details from under-12s.* You must not collect any personal details from or send any marketing to children under 12 years of age unless the child's parent or guardian has given explicit and provable consent to this. Subject to the conditions below, if the child's parent or guardian has given such consent you may collect such limited details from the child as you need to send him or her further limited mobile or online communications – name, age, mobile number and, if applicable, an e-mail address. You may only do this if you have first made clear to the child's parent or guardian, in such a way that the parent or guardian understands what is involved and has agreed to this, why you are requesting the child's details and what you are going to use them for.

2 *Use of children's details.* You may use these limited details for relationship marketing purposes provided that such marketing is appropriate to the age of the child and such use falls within the type of use that you have told the child's parent/guardian that you are going to use the child's details for. You must not make the child's details available to any third party unless you have explained why to the child's parent or guardian, and have obtained their explicit and provable consent to this.

Regulated products

If you are sending mobile marketing in relation to any specially regulated products or services – for example, insurance, tobacco, alcohol or gambling – then you must make sure that you comply with any specific legal or regulatory requirements in relation to the marketing of such products or services, and should take legal advice (where appropriate) regarding the targeted countries. If any sales are being entered into by consumers as part of a mobile marketing campaign so that there is no face-to-face contact between the consumer and the seller before the sale takes place, then there is specific legislation that may apply and you should take legal advice where appropriate.

If you are running a game, competition, prize promotion or prize draw, then you must include the requirement to obtain permission to enter from an adult or employer, and to provide proof of purchase. You will also need to consider:

- how and when winners will be notified
- any intention to involve winners in post-event publicity
- any conditions under which entries may be disqualified
- any costs that an entrant might not be expecting to pay in connection with the collection, delivery or use of the prize or item.

The laws that relate to lotteries and competitions are complex, and are different for almost every country. In particular, there is a risk that, if a campaign including an element that falls within these laws is not structured in the right way, you will be running an illegal lottery. If your campaign is going to include any game, competition, prize promotion or prize draw, then you must ensure that you comply with any additional legal requirements and should take legal advice where appropriate.

Skills and attributes of wireless marketers

The success of any marketing campaign is completely dependent on the execution, and on a team leader and experienced manager to monitor the success of the program and make immediate adjustments. It's OK to have a strategy in place, but you need somebody to manage and implement this strategy. The skills and attributes of just such a person are listed below, and – not surprisingly – they are nothing to do with technology but rather with good solid marketing skills.

Required skills and attributes include:

- excellent creativity and marketing skills
- the ability to communicate clearly and effectively, and to coordinate with a variety of teams

- strong analytical skills (forecasting, category trend analyses)
- strategic and critical thinking capabilities
- the proficiency to manage multiple complex projects concurrently
- strong vendor and external partner relationship skills
- problem-solving/solution-oriented skills
- the ability to work both individually and in a team environment
- the ability to thrive in a fast-paced and constantly evolving environment
- motivation and initiative.

Chapter 11
Adult content

In the last two years the adult mobile industry has been growing. You may already have started to hear about the lads down the pub showing off the adult content on their mobile phones – and because we wouldn't even think of taking an adult magazine out into public with us, erotica and mobile phones seem a match made in heaven. Adult entertainment on mobile phones is going mainstream, and with new content controls in place it has now become a legitimate, regulated industry. Adult mobile content opens up whole new imaginative experiences, and you can expect to see adult content the likes of which you'll never have seen before!

Mobile adult content has a number of factors that make commercial success appear to be inevitable. These include the following:

1 *Impulsivity*. As our mobiles are always with us, adult content is always access-ible. This offers the user an opportunity to buy on impulse, giving instant gratification.
2 *A non-committal payment system*. Adult services operating on a pay-per-view basis offer the mobile user an opportunity to check out adult content without making a commitment to a subscription or having to pay too much.
3 *Responsibility*. New content regulations that have been put in place (see later in this chapter) provide an approved audience for adult content so the scope for abuse is much lower. Users have confidence that, when they purchase 18+ content, it will be the real thing because of these regulations.
4 *Adult content works*. It is clear from the immense success of adult content on the Internet that it works, and because of this everyone will want a piece of the pie. This is going to lead to adult mobile content getting even more mainstream exposure, which can happen in a responsible fashion with the new content restrictions in place. Adult content is now not seen as something that is taboo,

peddled by dodgy vendors; it is a serious industry making serious sums of money.

5 *Innovation and personalization.* Adult content on mobile phones will be unlike adult content ever seen before; there is now the opportunity to engage the user on a one-to-one basis with personalized erotic content, to develop more and more immersive adult environments.

According to strategy analysts worldwide, handset users have already spent $400 million just on adult videos and pictures. Adult content as a whole on mobile phones generated global sales of $0.4bn (£208m) in 2004. Jupiter Research predicts that revenues from adult content will grow to around $2bn worldwide by 2009. The US porn industry generates between around $8bn and $10bn annually.

These figures clearly show that mobile porn is a dynamic industry that will grow, and they may be exceeded as the big adult entertainment houses start to take full advantage of mobile by developing their own portals and feeds.

So far, many of the erotic products we have seen have been simple adaptations of old content – such as images optimized for mobile handsets. As yet, nothing in the adult world has really pushed the boundaries of mobile entertainment; most of it has been designed to the technical limitations of low-specification handsets, or by people who don't really understand how to take advantage of mobile technology. However, it has sold really well, demonstrating the demand for wireless erotic content. Once content developers start really exploring the possibilities of mobile content with higher specification handsets, we can expect some very interesting, rich content.

Content controls

Mobile operators have a love–hate affair with adult content, and in the ongoing effort by mobile operators to stop children accessing information that they shouldn't see via mobile phones, the main operators have introduced a content rating system that is quite complicated. All operators realize the immense power of adult content to drive mobile data revenue, but if they were accused of helping children to gain access to this content it would be a disaster for them.

As discussed, adult content on mobile phones is now poised for a boom thanks to faster networks and next-generation handsets. Adult content pioneers are beginning to harness this new technology to benefit customers for monetary gain. Selling sex on telephones through chat lines has become a main source of income for the industry, and now the possibility of sending high-resolution images, long videos and one-to-one video messaging, and giving the user access to community-style content, has become a reality. *Playboy*, for one, has already sold the rights for its pin-ups through mobile phones, and it has been joined by many other content providers, such as the *Daily Sport* and Vivid Entertainment.

There have been a few attempts at barring adult data, but this has led to legitimate services being blocked as well. The new content rules make the content suppliers responsible for rating the content themselves, whether it is adult or non-adult, which works in the same way as age restrictions on a film or video game. Different operators have adopted different policies on adult content from a user's point of view; Vodafone, for example, barred all phones from adult services and asked users to phone up or register on the Internet to prove that they were over 18. Many saw this as the end of the road for adult content suppliers, but it has had the reverse effect and sales are reported to have grown across the adult mobile industry since Vodafone made this decision in January 2004. This growth points to a gradual awakening to the fact that there is a way of offering mobile erotica in a responsible way; as a result of access controls, less reputable companies who were adopting tricky and underhand tactics to sell their adult content (for example, promoting it to children) have now been weeded out.

Content controls around the world

Wireless adult products are already big business in Asia and Europe, where consumers of mobile-based adult content spend an average of US$34 per year downloading erotic images and explicit videos. However, suppliers need to take care to conform to local regulations: different policies apply in each country, and even within a country operators enforce widely different rules. China, for example, has targeted the telephone-sex industry, severely punishing anyone who offers the service. Table 11.1 provides a brief breakdown of how mobile content is controlled in various countries; this is only a rough guideline and rules may change, so further research is advised if you are planning to sell adult content in one of the mentioned countries.

UK adult content controls in depth

In the UK, content controls have been introduced by the mobile operators so that anyone who wants to access adult rated content will first have to age verify. This section explains the process for Vodafone, Orange, T-Mobile and O2, and what each has done to meet the voluntary Code of Practice that restricts the availability of unsuitable content to customers under the age of 18 years. An example of a company that can handle the process of unblocking content is Bango (www.bango.net), which has been appointed as an independent classification body for adult content (Figure 11.1).

Table 11.1 *Adult content controls around the world*

Country	Adult content restrictions	Adult chat allowed?	Conditions
Austria	Yes, with conditions	Yes, with conditions	For premium services costing 1€ or more per message, the end-user must be able to request the service via a standard price MO message. Adult pornographic services are forbidden on Telering
Belgium	Yes, on dedicated shortcodes only	Yes, on dedicated shortcodes only	Customer must sign the Code of Conduct. Adult services must run on dedicated shortcodes
Denmark	No	No	Adult services forbidden
Finland	Yes	Yes	Read operators' general rules carefully; there are no specific guidelines
France	Yes, with conditions	Yes, with conditions	Generally, soft erotic services are acceptable but harder pornography is forbidden. Each service should be accurately described and presented to operators before launch
Germany	No	Yes, with conditions	Peer-to-peer adult chat is allowed. The mainstream German market is, in general, trying to move away from anything seen as explicit
Hungary	No	No	Only allowed to run three categories of services: TV voting, information, and registration game (i.e. competition)
Ireland	No	No	Adult services are forbidden
Italy	No	No	Adult services are forbidden
Mexico	No	No	Adult services are forbidden
Netherlands	Yes	Yes	Customer must sign Code of Conduct. Subscription services must be explained clearly
Poland	Yes, with conditions	Yes, with conditions	Only 'soft' adult services are allowed
Portugal	Yes, with conditions	Yes, with conditions	Adult services must be explicitly advertised as 'Content for people above 18'

Spain	Yes, with conditions	Yes, with conditions	Services are strictly one MO to one MT; revenue will not be paid if MOs and MTs do not balance.
Sweden	Yes, with conditions	Yes, with conditions	Customer must check and comply with Ethic Charter/Code of Conduct. Marketing for adult services shall not provide procurement for sexual services, or contain any reference to/involvement of under–18s. In the daily press, TV, radio or direct marketing, no indications of sexual acts or occurrences, sexual violence, sadism or cruelty are allowed; on printed support, no display photos or drawings/other illustrations portraying sexual or erotic material are allowed
Switzerland	Yes, with conditions	Yes, with conditions	'Soft' erotic services are OK but pornographic services are very strictly regulated. The classification of content is carried out subjectively by each operator. Pornographic services require extensive independent legal advice/sign-off before an operator will let it run on their network
UK	Yes, with conditions	Yes, with conditions	Adult chat services require prior permission from ICSTIS and must be run strictly according to the certificate. In general, content that can be bought in a shop is OK but anything which is more explicit requires special consideration

Figure 11.1 *The Bango website (www.bango.net) – reproduced with permission*

The UK Code of Practice

The voluntary code of practice restricts the availability of unsuitable content to customers under the age of 18 years. The code provides an independent classification body to classify material as '18', consistent with standards used by other media. The main measures of the Mobile Content Code of Practice are as follows:

- All adult material will be classified '18' and the operators will make sure that mobile phone users have been age verified before they can access such material
- Commercial chat rooms will only be accessible by those who are over 18, or must be moderated to make sure they are not used improperly
- Parents and bill-payers are offered the opportunity to apply filters to block access by phone users to adult content on the Internet
- Mobile phone operators will work with the police and authorities to combat the distribution of illegal material, and will also work together to combat bulk nuisance communications
- The mobile phone operators will work to provide advice and raise people's awareness about how to use their mobile phones to avoid unwelcome contact and protect users from undesirable material.

140

Barring a mobile

Following the UK Operator Code of Practice, parents can now bar their children's mobile phones from accessing adult content. This is done through Bango. To do this, the parent needs to:

1 Text the message 'go bar' to 87121. The message costs £1.50, and when it has been sent a confirmation message will be received along with a WAP push message to take them to the Bango WAP site, where they can bar the phone.
2 Enter the url: bango.net/bar on the mobile phone and go to the WAP site, then follow the on-screen instructions to bar the phone.

Doing this inserts a 'barred' tag into the user identity database for that phone, and if the user then tries to access adult content a look-up is made against the phone and the barred tag is detected. Parents can unbar the phone at a later date by entering a unique unbarring code.

UK operator content controls
O2 content controls

- Age verification is required for 18-rated content; this can be done either via WAP or in store. Age verification is done via credit card and against the electoral role.
- There is no cost to the user to age verify. The user is charged £1 but is given £1.50 to buy mobile content. The age-verification process is managed by Bango.
- Phone users (such as parents) can filter 18 content by calling 61818. This activates a whitelist, and the user is then only able to browse the O2 active portal.

Orange content controls

- Age verification is required for 18-rated content; this is done via WAP.
- There is no cost to the user to age verify. To age verify, the user is asked for their credit card details. The user is charged 10p and this amount is then automatically refunded to their credit card. The credit card statement shows this transaction, plus the phone number of Orange Customer Service. The age-verification process is managed by Bango.
- Phone users will be able to filter 18 content (no details are present).

T-Mobile content controls

- Age verification is required for 18-rated content; this is done via WAP.
- The user age verifies either using a credit card or via an identity check.

- There are no details at present regarding whether users will have to pay to age verify.
- T-Mobile has already built an opted-in list of users.
- All content will be filtered, and 18 content hidden behind content controls. The filter will not automatically block content that it cannot read, such as an executable (games, video, polyphonic ring tone). This content will be blocked if it is found to contain adult content.

Vodafone content controls

- Age verification is required for 18-rated content. This is done via WAP, in store, at the Vodafone website or by calling customer service.
- The user age verifies using either a credit card or an identity check at a Vodafone store.
- The user is charged £1 and receives an airtime credit of £2.50.
- All content is filtered and 18 content is hidden behind content controls. The filter automatically blocks content it cannot read, such as an executable (games, video, polyphonic ring tone).
- Content providers need to submit any universal content to the Vodafone whitelist to ensure their site is not blocked, or to unblock one that the filter has detected.

Adult bar codes

A great example of an innovative combination of mobile technology and adult content has come from Vivid Entertainment, one of the top suppliers of adult content worldwide. Vivid has licensed a system that lets shoppers preview trailers of their videos on their handsets by scanning the bar code on the box with their phone. To see the clips, users must download a small application from Vivid's website that works on Internet-enabled camera phones or PCs with a webcam. In a shop the user takes a picture of the bar code with their phone through the application; this bar code includes an embedded URL, and the phone's screen is redirected to a website that hosts the clips. None of the clips contain sex or nudity, so can be downloaded to the handset without restrictions. The technology is called *Leapscan*®, and has been licensed from a company called xobile.

Conclusion

The growth of adult content is clearly inevitable, and the regulation introduced at this early stage means that mobile adult entertainment will become a legitimate industry, far removed from the unregulated world of the Internet. With the advances in technology, greater bandwidth and more widespread use of more powerful handsets, mobile erotic content is set to bloom, with the successful players being those who are offering something worth viewing on a handset. The key will be to give consumers real value for money, and to deliver products and experiences that they can't access anywhere else.

Chapter 12

Application environments

Wireless applications, from simple applications to complicated 3G games, need a platform to run on – a software system that interprets the application instructions and tells the device how to execute them.

For application developers, the more standardized that platform can be the better, because it means they can address a larger market with lower development costs. However, a number of rival platforms and standards have made life difficult for mobile application developers; they have had to pick up new skills and development techniques quickly in order to cater for the range of environments and of handsets they work on.

The current market leader is a flavour of Sun Microsystems' Java programming language, Java 2 Platform, Micro Edition – or J2ME. Almost every handset maker supports J2ME, including Nokia, Samsung, Sony Ericsson and Motorola. Other development environments of note are Symbian, BREW and Flash Lite.

J2ME

J2ME started with one version of Java, which is now known as Java 2 Standard Edition (J2SE), and that had the tagline 'Write Once, Run Anywhere^{TM}'. The idea behind Java was to create a language that would enable developers to write their own code once, which would then run on any platform that supported a Java Virtual Machine. Java was launched in 1995; it originally only worked on desktop machines, but has since extended its reach much further. Java 2 Enterprise Edition (J2EE) has been launched to provide support for enterprise-wide applications, and the most recent edition of the language is Java 2 Micro Edition (J2ME), which was launched to target 'information appliances' – most notably mobile phones.

Figure 12.1 *The Sun Developer Network website (java.sun.com)*

A great website to check out for the latest updates in Java technology is the Sun Developer Network site at http://java.sun.com/ (Figure 12.1).

To summarize, available Java editions include:

- the Standard Edition (J2SE), which was designed to run on desktop and workstation computers
- the Enterprise Edition (J2EE), which has built-in support for Servlets, JSP and XML, and is aimed at server-based applications

- the Micro Edition (J2ME), which was designed for devices with limited memory, display and processing power.

Why Choose J2ME?

J2ME is a flexible environment, aimed solely at consumer devices with limited processing power. With the introduction of J2ME, devices have been able to download applications and games to extend their functionality; they no longer need to be 'static' in nature. Java as a programming language is easy to master, and its environment is secure and portable, with access to dynamic content and a huge developer community of over two million people. The Micro Edition of Java was developed to address the special needs of consumer devices, and as such does not contain all the functionality of J2SE or J2EE; current hand-held devices do not have the capabilities to cope with this functionality, although as handsets get more powerful in the future this will change.

The capabilities of devices within the Micro Edition may vary greatly. A PDA will have a much larger screen size than a pager, and you will need to take this into consideration when developing content in Java. Even devices that are similar in size may vary greatly in their capabilities, depending on the screen resolution, what version of J2ME they support, and the available memory and processing power. To accommodate the range of devices that support Java, a number of configurations and profiles have been introduced.

J2ME configurations

Sun introduced the configuration to support the broad range of products that fit within the scope of J2ME. A configuration defines a Java platform, and is closely tied to a Java Virtual Machine (JVM). The configuration defines the features and core Java libraries of the JVM. The deciding factors as to what configuration applies to which phone are usually memory, display, the limits of network connectivity, and the raw processing power of that device.

Here are the typical characteristics of devices within the two currently defined configurations:

1 Connected Device Configuration (CDC)

- 512 kilobytes (minimum) of memory for running Java
- 256 kilobytes (minimum) for runtime memory allocation
- network connectivity, possibly persistent and high bandwidth.

2 Connected, Limited Device Configuration (CLDC)

- 128 kilobytes of memory for running Java
- 32 kilobytes of memory for runtime memory allocation
- restricted user interface
- low power, typically battery powered
- network connectivity, typically wireless, with low bandwidth and inter-mittent access.

The division between these two configurations is quite clear, but with the advance of mobile technology it is expected to blur.

J2ME profiles

PDAs and mobile phones may fall into the same configuration, but there also needs to be flexibility within the configuration to take advantage of the particular features of each device. To cope with this, Sun also introduced profiles within the configurations to allow for flexibility into the future as technology advances. A profile is an extension of a configuration. It provides the libraries for a developer to write applications for a particular type of device. An example of a profile is the Mobile Information Device Profile (MIDP), which defines APIs for the user interface, network capabilities and storage.

Java Virtual Machine (JVM)

The engine behind a Java application is the JVM. The JVM translates the class files (included in the Java Archive File – JAR) into the code for the platform running the JVM – the mobile device, in this case. The JVM provides security and manages memory; it is essentially what makes Java programs function. For CLDC devices Sun has developed the K Virtual Machine (KVM); designed to handle the constraints and special considerations of mobile devices, it has the following key features:

- the virtual machine itself requires only 40–80 kilobytes of memory
- only 20–40 kilobytes of dynamic memory (heap) are required
- it can run on 16-bit processors clocked at only 25 MHz.

Will J2SE applications run on J2ME?

J2ME is basically a slimmed-down version of J2SE, with many components removed to keep the platform small and efficient. If you write J2SE code that only adheres to the classes in the J2ME configuration, then your programs will work on both platforms but will appear very limited on the J2SE device because of the restrictions of the J2ME environment.

J2ME advantages

J2ME provides a powerful foundation for content developers, with:

- easy migration from existing content
- an abundant network of Java developers, which means a readily available workforce
- linking between wired and wireless services
- excellent security functions
- graphical user interfaces
- the ability to function offline
- peer-to-peer networking
- over the air application downloads
- widespread handset support.

Java content examples

Sprite Java Magazine

The Java Magazine (Figure 12.2) is highly customizable, allowing for re-branding, the different requirements of each user and the brand experience. The application was designed to be delivered via WAP to any WAP/Java-enabled handsets.

Figure 12.2 *The Sprite Java Magazine – reproduced with permission*

Each magazine contains a graphical splash screen and menu screen and up to eight fixed content areas as standard; each content area contains up to two sub-screens of content. Content on a lower level has no rich graphics, but can contain a header and links to download content.

Each magazine is a stand-alone application. The interface and content are fully customizable, and each magazine has strong graphical and animated elements with integrated sound and vibration. Each brand experience is a new compilation.

Services that can be triggered from within each magazine are as follows:

- each page in the magazine can contain a ticker-tape to provide the user with up-to-date information and offers
- ring-tone and wallpaper purchases can be made through shortcode or direct from button selection
- alerts, subscriptions and unsubscriptions can be activated through a shortcode or direct from a button selection
- competitions can be entered through a shortcode or direct from a button selection
- there is SMS feedback submission
- voting is from a button selection, with up-to-the-minute results presented from within the application
- a locally run quiz can be entered, with a dial out to a WAP site for hints and tips on the answers
- the user clicks to an external WAP session.

MatchMaker

We developed the MatchMaker (Figure 12.3) as part of the lifestyle range of Java applications. Using technology based on natural biorhythms, we created a tool to match the user to his or her perfect partner. Based on both dates of birth, the user is told how physically, emotionally and intellectually compatible they are with their partner, and given an overall compatibility reading.

Users can also use the MatchMaker to check their own natural biorhythms and see when their periods of peak performance will be, including power days! If they want to see how compatible they are with their favourite celebrities, then, by using the 'celeb match', they can run a check to see how they would get on with over 200 celebrities – from David Beckham to Kate Winslet.

We also decided to include an advice section – The Love Guru, which functions like a magic eight-ball. There is also a fun 'Love Scanner' (Figure 12.4), which can

Figure 12.3 *MatchMaker – reproduced with permission*

Figure 12.4 *The Love Scanner – reproduced with permission*

be used to check out a potential partner. Lastly we added a Name Checker, based on the science of numerology, to find out what a user's name says about him or her, and how compatible the user's name is with their partner's.

MatchMaker was designed to appeal to a mixed audience, and it has a primarily female user base. The application has been designed to be eye-catching, with just the right amount of throw-away fun and seriousness.

Love Scanner

The Love Scanner was developed as an extension of the MatchMaker application, following its success. It is a photo-matching application. A user loads up the Scanner with his or her photo, lines up a potential partner in the viewfinder and clicks away. Once the user has photographed the potential partner the Love Scanner runs, comparing the user's photo to that of the potential partner using our advanced biometric scanning processes. Once the scan is complete the user is given a compatibility statement for that person, and can then store the photo and scan and e-mail it to friends or to him- or herself, with a personal message of the user's choosing. We also made it a bit racier by including the option to scan other body parts, which has proved to be a point of great interest.

Love Scanner only works on phones that are MIDP 2 compatible because of the functions needed to trigger the camera from within a Java application. It is the first application of its kind, and appeals to a young audience, both male and female. The navigation around the application has been designed to be intuitive and colourful and the e-mail scanning introduces a viral element to the application, with footers placed on the bottom of each e-mail prompting the recipient to download the application.

Pub Fun Duck Shoot

Pub Fun Duck Shoot (Figure 12.5) was developed as one of the Pub Fun range of products, which have proved very successful. The aim was to develop a Java game with rich graphics and sound to appeal to as wide an audience as possible. The graphics in Pub Fun Duck Shoot were all 3D rendered before going into the game to make them as rich as possible, and real sounds were used for the ducks quacking and rifle shots to create a more immersive playing environment. The graphics were kept in a 'cartoon' style to keep the action light-hearted in nature. Based on the classic duck hunt game, Pub Fun Duck Shoot has proved very popular since its launch; there are three difficulty levels to keep even the most hardened gamer happy, and its trademark 'Doom for Ducks!' tagline has helped it to become our top-selling game from the Pub Fun range.

Figure 12.5 *Pub Fun Duck Shoot – reproduced with permission*

DSA Theory Test

The DSA Theory Test was one of the first applications that we developed across 2.5G and 3G. There are two versions of the application; one standard version for 2.5G handsets and one enhanced version featuring the ten official hazard perception practice clips from the UK Driving Standards Authority, allowing the user to get used to the hazard perception test before taking it for real.

The test contains up-to-the-minute questions from the actual theory test, presented in a quiz format. It is the ideal learning tool for people taking the theory test, or drivers wanting to brush up on their knowledge of the many signs and systems on the road today. Questions are presented in a multiple-choice format, and answers are given after each question for effective learning. Our unique quiz format was used to add a fun, interactive element to the test, the randomly generated questions appearing in groups of ten. Once a group of ten has been answered correctly, the questions are cleared from the database and the user moves on to the next ten. If users get a question wrong they have to start another group of ten randomly chosen questions. The aim is to answer all the questions correctly. Developing 2.5G and 3G versions of the application meant maximum handset compatibility and appealed to many of the network operators who needed innovative, branded content for their 3G portals.

Figure 12.6 *The DSA Theory Test – reproduced with permission*

Mobile Business Tools Suite

Eighty per cent of business people carry colour mobile phones (a number that is growing all the time), and around 70 per cent of these handsets are Java enabled. We saw the need for a universal set of business applications to cover the range of phones on the market, and Java was the ideal language to program these in to ensure maximum compatibility. The 'My Business' range of applications was developed to simplify the life of a business mobile phone user, and the eight products were developed alongside a web interface, taking a feed from one single data source, so users could access the same data on their mobile phone as on the web. This is updated with a 'synchronize' button on the handset and on the web.

The applications in the suite are:

1 My Accounts
2 My Business
3 My Expense Tracker
4 My Mileage Tracker
5 My Check Book
6 My Safe
7 My Golf Card
8 My Time Tracker.

Figure 12.7 *My Safe and My Check Book – reproduced with permission*

We have also developed enterprise versions of the applications for a number of clients. My Safe has proved especially popular for this use; each employee in a company is issued a version of My Safe with company-specific codes and passwords in it, and these can be updated on a company-wide basis whenever a password changes, keeping all relevant employees up to date.

3G Travel guides

The 3G donTmiss city guides were developed as a follow-up to our original donTmiss city guides. We had originally developed guides to the top 45 cities in the world, including information on the best places to see, top restaurants, and a survival kit for each city, with key phrases and phone numbers. The original guides proved very successful across a number of operators and aggregators, so we took the top five cities – London, Paris, Barcelona, Dublin and Venice – and developed a 3G version for each. The cities were London, Paris, Barcelona.

Each guide has the top six tourist destinations with in–depth commentary on each, and a panoramic guide that allows the user to pan around and view the destination and local area. Because of the size of these panoramics and the depth of the rest of the content available, it was decided to develop the applications to run on only 3G handsets. We took advantage of the 3G environment further by incorporating a gallery feature with high-resolution photographs of 30 other destinations in

Figure 12.8 *donTmiss 3G city guide for London – reproduced with permission*

each city; these are stored online and are pulled through dynamically to the handset when a user chooses to view them, allowing us to update them when we like. Each city guide also contains a detailed restaurant guide, a survival kit, and a phrasebook that features essential words and phrases organized by subject for every situation and combined with a simple pronunciation guide. The depth of content available in each of the guides has led to them becoming a success on a number of operator portals around the world.

Mobile pets

'Mobile pets' has been one of our top performing range of products. We originally developed the pets in 2002, and now have a library of over fifteen. Many operators and aggregators take all the pets to be featured on their portal as a 'mobile pets' category, and their simplicity and 'stickiness' have been the keys to their success over the years. Each pet runs in a Java application, and while the user is away from the pet it will get hungry, tired, unhappy or dirty; the aim is to give each pet a balanced enough lifestyle to make sure it stays with you for a long time. We also developed a 'second generation' of gaming pets, which includes a fun game. The better the user looks after the pet the better it will perform in the game, and this links up to the Sprite Wired platform, an online scoreboard where users can compare their scores against one another.

Figure 12.9 *Cuddles and Pebbles mobile pets – reproduced with permission*

We have also been approached by a number of companies to build exclusive pets, including the Crazy Frog pet for Jamba and the Inspector Gadget pet for Jetix (Fox Kids). The pets will go on into the future with SMS feedback from within the application and pet communities, where users' pets can interact with one another to win prizes. Watch this space!

Mobile Survival Kit

The Mobile Survival Kit was developed to be an essential application that every mobile phone user should have. By giving a Java application multiple functionality, the Survival Kit provides value for money and a number of great tools that are not available elsewhere. It contains the following:

1 *Massager*. The massager uses the vibration function of your phone for self-applied massage. There are different settings for a range of applications, from deep, continuous muscle toning to short-burst stress relief. The massager has the following default settings:

- gentle caress
- continuous
- burst

Figure 12.10 *The Mobile Survival Kit – reproduced with permission*

- falling
- rising
- random.

You can also program your own vibrations to your phone; we added a risqué element to the marketing of this part of the application by stating 'Why limit it to yourself, massage your friends and partners for maximum fun!'

2 *Torch Light.* Light up the screen of your handset with the Torch Light. You can set the colour of your torch, and make it flash, either to one of our pre-defined flashing patterns or by programming your own. It's great for reading, parties and nightclubs!

3 *Code Safe.* Store your bank account, card, computer password log-in and any other sensitive information on your phone in a safe password-protected environment. This uses a stripped down version of the My Safe engine.

4 *World Clock.* Check the time in more than 300 locations worldwide, including weekday and date for each location. World Clock features four independent clocks to enable you to compare times simultaneously on one screen. With automatic daylight-saving time calculation and customizable locations, World Clock is the ultimate traveller's companion.

5 *Birthday List.* Never forget a birthday again! Enter your friends' birthdays into the calendar and set how far in advance you want to be reminded, then

whenever you open the application you'll get a reminder telling you whose birthdays are coming up. You can also view the calendar over any range of dates for a complete birthday overview. This was the closest we could get to doing a full birthday application from within a Java application. As the functionality of Java develops, we expect to see birthday-list type applications with automatic reminders and SMS reminders being developed.

6 *TxtSpeak Dictionary.* This is the ultimate text messaging dictionary, where you can check out over 200 cheeky phrases and abbreviations. The TxtSpeak Dictionary gives you the power to understand all the emoticons and abbreviations, perfect for you to save time and wind up your friends.

The Mobile Survival Kit was an ambitious project that has been widely accepted by content aggregators and operators. Different versions with different levels of graphics have been developed so it works on as many handsets as possible, but the core functionality and value for money still remain throughout each handset version.

Symbian

What is Symbian?

Symbian OS is a phone operating system and development environment. It is currently owned by Ericsson, Panasonic, Nokia, Samsung, Siemens and Sony Ericsson. There are a number of different phones with different user interfaces that use the Symbian OS, such as UIQ and the 60 series Nokia handsets. Symbian can be used on a wide range of devices, from clam-shell phones to PDAs. Symbian is structured like many standard desktop operating systems, and has such features as multitasking, multithreading and memory protection. Symbian was built to be a robust platform for hand-held devices, with a strong emphasis on memory management and disk space conservation; the unique features to keep memory usage low mean that high-performance applications and games can be developed on modest hardware. All Symbian OS programming is event-based, and the CPU is switched off when applications are not dealing with an event; this allows the battery life of Symbian handsets to be extended considerably.

Symbian allows you to develop native applications. The Symbian installations system (SIS) supports over the air installation so the delivery of these applications is not a problem, although Symbian applications can be quite big in size so desktop installation (by Bluetooth or serial cable) is usually the preferred method. Native applications running on Symbian OS have much better access to device hardware and software than J2ME applications, and performance is significantly better because of this. Symbian uses C++ as a native programming language. This makes it quite hard to program in comparison to J2ME, but there are a number of Software Development Kits (SDKs) available to help with Symbian development. A great source of information for the Symbian developer is The Symbian Developer Network (at http://www.symbian.com).

Flash Lite

What is Macromedia Flash Lite?

Macromedia Flash Lite is a new version of Flash Player that has been developed specifically for mobile phones. Mobile phones currently do not have the processing power available to support the standard Flash Player, so this cut-down version was produced. With Flash Lite, mobile phone users can enjoy rich multimedia content on their mobiles, and it opens up the mobile development space to the millions of Flash developers around the world. Flash Lite 1.1 (the current edition) uses Flash 4 ActionScript, which keeps the file size and processor requirements small. As handsets become more powerful, expect to see this support become more advanced. Flash Lite offers many opportunities for developers to create animated and data-driven content that will be in high demand in the near future. Flash Lite support on handsets is, so far, limited, but expect to see it become widespread in the future, Macromedia is working with a number of handset manufacturers, including i-mode, Nokia, Samsung and Motorola, to ensure that Flash will be supported on their handsets into the future – so it is a key development area. The key source on the web for Flash Lite related information is the Macromedia website (http://www.macromedia.com).

Developer tips

Flash Lite content is compiled in the same way as standard Flash content, as an swf file that then has to be transferred to the handset – usually by desktop transfer (Bluetooth or serial cable). We have noticed a few important points that should be considered when developing Flash Lite 1.1 content. You'll need to keep an eye on CPU-intensive operations. Always look at the performance of the phone you're developing, for the following can severely impair the performance of Flash Lite movies on your phone:

- too many alpha and gradation settings
- simultaneous tweening of multiple symbols
- embedded fonts
- complex ActionScript.

To optimize your movies, make sure you test them on all target phones prior to deployment, and experiment with different ways of creating animations – particularly via ActionScript. Flash Lite supports device fonts and embedded fonts, but if you use embedded fonts you will notice that your file size will rocket. You need to keep an eye on the size of your swf file at all times. Flash Lite differs from standard Flash in that it does not support streaming playback, so the user will only see your movie once it has completely loaded; in the case of large files, this could mean a long wait. There are several ways to keep your file size down, including using movie clips rather than graphic symbols, using device fonts and optimizing your paths (Modify > Shape > Optimize in Flash MX Professional 2004). There is a fine balance to strike between file size and functionality, and it changes from handset to handset. The best way to find that balance is to experiment with your content and make sure you test it on as wide a range of handsets as possible.

FlashCast

FlashCast has been developed by Macromedia as a client-server solution for the creation of rich data services, adding to the functionality of Flash Lite and making it a fully networkable development environment. The FlashCast server uses the Flash Lite engine to enable a number of network features. FlashCast can be used for live content updates within a Flash application, which is ideal for magazine-style content. Also, by caching channel data on a handset, FlashCast ensures an 'always on' experience – even in areas where there is no signal.

The FlashCast service is managed and delivered by a carrier-grade server hosted by the mobile operator; this server manages tasks such as subscription accounts, billing transactions and content updates. FlashCast updates using SMS, HTTP or UDP, giving it a high level of flexibility.

BREW

BREW is an application development environment created by Qualcomm for CDMA-based mobile phones. BREW stands for Binary Runtime Environment for Wireless; it runs at the firmware level and specially targets wireless applications that can be downloaded and executed on mobile devices. The environment is available free of charge to CDMA device manufacturers, and it works in a similar way to the virtual machine in Java. The fact that it runs at chipset level means that BREW can tap into the communication and multimedia capabilities of mobile devices in a more effective way than can J2ME. As part of the BREW application platform, Qualcomm offers a BREW porting kit; a BREW SDK that provides development tools, documentation, APIs, etc.; and a BREW distribution system. The website to check out for BREW information is the Qualcomm website (www.qualcomm.com/brew/).

The BREW distribution system

Qualcomm offer a unique distribution system for BREW content. Qualcomm's solution manages all the distribution and billing issues, and developers get their share of revenue for their applications downloaded by users of a network. Before an application is available for download it has to be approved by Qualcomm; this certification provides a level of security for end-users, who can be sure they are getting a quality product, and it ensures a communication network is set up with developers, so feedback on products can be managed efficiently. The main strength of BREW is that this business model is simple and works for developers. BREW is not known for being easy to develop for, but it can be very lucrative because of the way Qualcomm controls it. Qualcomm sets the revenue share for the operators, as well as all the billing and settlement, and makes it very easy for users to buy applications, as well as imposing rules on how much their creators are paid.

In order to create BREW applications you need the BREW SDK, which can be downloaded from the Qualcomm website, and an Arm Compiler. The BREW environment is based on C++, like Symbian. For some operators you may also need to pass a testing procedure called TRUE BREW® before your applications will be accepted. Once an application has been accepted it is posted onto the BREW operator extranet, and from here operators can see it and decide whether they want to adopt it for their network. Qualcomm also allow you to monitor downloads of your product from their website.

To a user, BREW presents a similar experience to Java; however, they are very different in core philosophy. While J2ME looks to enable developers to write applications with maximum compatibility, BREW only works on certain handsets and therefore lacks portability – but this results in enhanced performance on these handsets. When deciding which way to go, Java or BREW, you should consider which handsets and operators you will be targeting and then work from there. Both environments have their advantages, but ultimately you will be driven by how many handsets you want to reach with your products. So far BREW has not broken into the market in Europe, and support is mainly concentrated in the USA (their largest customer is the Verizon network), but expect to see the BREW operating system integrated into handsets released in Europe soon – especially since Qualcomm has recently announced that the BREW operating system now supports Java, much like Symbian.

Chapter 13

WAP and the mobile Internet

The Wireless Application Protocol (WAP) is an open specification that enables mobile users to access and interact with information and services. WAP was developed by the WAP Forum, an industry group set up in 1997, which has now been consolidated into the Open Mobile Alliance (OMA).

The Open Mobile Alliance

The OMA was formed in June 2002 by nearly 200 companies, including mobile operators, device manufacturers, and content and service providers. The OMA aims to represent the whole mobile value chain, and consolidate into one organization all specification activities in the mobile world (Figure 13.1). The OMA has a number of goals:

1 To deliver high-quality, open technical specifications based upon market requirements that drive modularity, extensibility and consistency amongst enablers to reduce industry implementation efforts
2 To ensure that OMA service enabler specifications provide interoperability across different devices, geographies, service providers, operators and networks, to facilitate interoperability of the resulting product implementations
3 To be the catalyst for the consolidation of standards activity within the mobile data service industry; working in conjunction with other existing standards organizations and the industry to improve interoperability and decrease operational costs for all involved
4 To provide value and benefits to members in OMA from all parts of the value chain, including content and service providers, information technology providers, mobile operators and wireless vendors, such that they elect actively to participate in the organization.

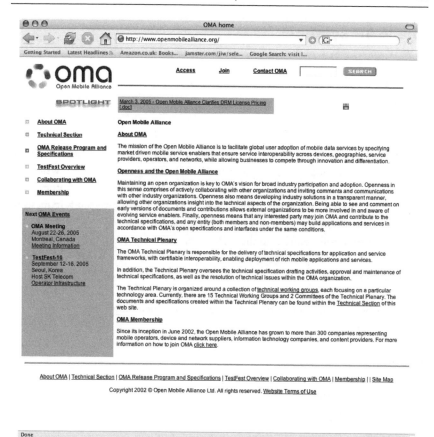

Figure 13.1 *The OMA website (www.openmobilealliance.org)*

(Source: The OMA website, http://www.openmobilealliance.org/about_OMA/index.html).

WAP works in a similar way to the Internet – users can view WAP sites from many different companies and individuals with a range of content. A lot of things available on the Internet are also available on WAP. Phones are slower, smaller and have less memory than PCs, so WAP was designed to maximize the experience of Internet applications within the restricted environment of the mobile phone. WAP is a communications protocol and application environment and can be built on any operating system, including PalmOS, EPOC, Windows CE, FLEXOS, OS/9 and JavaOS. Products that support WAP include digital wireless devices such as mobile phones, pagers, two-way radios, smart phones and communicators. WAP is designed to work with most wireless networks, such as CDPD, CDMA, GSM, PDC, PHS, TDMA, FLEX, ReFLEX, iDEN, TETRA, DECT, DataTAC and Mobitex.

The WAP system

A WAP enabled system consists of:

- a WAP gateway
- an HTTP web server
- a WAP device.

The WAP gateway is a mediator between a WAP device and an HTTP or HTTPS server; it routes requests from the WAP device to the server. When the HTTP server receives a request from the WAP gateway, it sends this information to the device using a wireless network. The WAP device in turn sends requests to the WAP gateway, which translates WAP requests to web requests, allowing the WAP client to submit requests to the web server. After receiving the response from the server, the WAP gateway translates web responses into WAP responses or a format understood by the WAP client, and sends it to the WAP device.

WAP can be used for lots of different applications, including:

- e-mail
- shopping
- news reports
- travel information
- checking share prices
- checking weather
- entertainment news and views
- horoscopes
- to download or to play online games
- sports reports
- chat rooms.

For companies or individuals wishing to monetize their content in the mobile space, launching a WAP site or mobile browsing service is essential. Mobile browsing provides a stand-alone medium on which companies can promote their services, and WAP sites provide a great opportunity to market and sell content and services to a massive audience. Many companies are rushing to build their WAP sites, but are realizing that it's not as simple as creating a mobile version of a website.

WAP pages are designed to be viewed on the small screens of a phone, so they generally don't have lots of graphics or colours. The basic operation is quite similar to that of simple web pages – users view a page, and on the page there generally are a number of links to other pages (Figure 13.2). Users select the link they want to follow by scrolling to it and clicking a button on their handset.

Figure 13.2 *The WapJam WAP site – reproduced with permission*

WAP design guidelines

Mobile Internet sites are not as easy to use or develop as their computer-oriented website cousins, owing to the smaller screens, text input via a keypad, and many different user situations. Severe design mistakes continue to be made in WAP site development; we have seen this a number of times and have put together a set of guidelines for site development that will make sure your mobile Internet site will be accessible and usable.

An unusable site will prevent users from being able to perform even the most simple of tasks. Sites need to be rational and contain relevant content that is easy to browse through. One of the most important areas to consider with WAP site development, as with website development, is information architecture. A well-designed information architecture will enable users to find information quickly and in a rational, well thought-out way; it is the key to having a usable site. Before building your site, take the time to sit down and plan it out – where the links will be, what areas the site will contain, which areas contain what content and so on. This may seem obvious, but it will give you the structure to be able to build your site in a logical way. The information architecture provides the skeleton to build the rest of the site on, and even the most simple of sites needs thinking out before you start designing and building it.

Websites generally aid the user with some kind of navigation bar, which will provide links to the key areas in the site as well as back to the homepage. Backwards navigation is another area you will need to consider carefully when developing a WAP site, as users frequently want to return to the page they have just visited.

PDA navigation

When designing a mobile Internet site for a PDA or small computer such as a Pocket PC or Palm, the device's browser will usually have a built in back button like a desktop browser. There are a couple of main rules of thumb to be considered when developing a site for a PDA; these are only general, but will help you develop a user-friendly site.

1 Avoid navigation bars, as these will take up too much real estate on the screen. Instead, you should use information in a 'tree' format to identify where the user is in the site – for example, Home > Games > Action.
2 Avoid the use of 'back' links, as users will have to find them and they will take up valuable space on the screen. As mentioned before, the device's browser will usually have a 'back' button and you can prompt the user to go back using the navigation system outlined in point (1) above.

Figure 13.3 shows the Voltimum WAP site on a PDA, developed by Sprite.

Top tips for WAP

WAP is a flexible medium and, like all media, works best when the content is tailored specifically to it and takes advantage of its many attributes. Here are some general tips for creating a user-friendly, efficient WAP site; they are by no means set in stone, as each project will be unique, but provide a set of rules for creating a solid site, whatever the brief.

Splash screens

Splash screens should be avoided as a general rule. If you are only developing a site for a high-speed audience (3G) then you can include a screen, as the download time will be that much less, but on slower networks splash screens add a lot of time to the experience because users have to download a large image before they can begin browsing your site. This will associate your brand with time wasting, and it is also possible that large images will cause problems on lower-specification handsets.

Figure 13.3 *The Voltimum WAP site on a PDA, developed by Sprite*

Think about your navigation

As mentioned previously, strong information architecture is the key to a strong site, whether a website or a WAP site. Ensure the user can go 'back' from every page, as not all handsets have back buttons. It is a sure way to lose customers if they cannot get to where they want to go, or they get lost whilst navigating around your site. They should be able to return to the main homepage with one click from wherever they are in the site. One great way of keeping your users on track is to give each of the links in the site a number; this makes it easier for users to recognize the link the further they go into the site, and it differentiates between links. Make sure each link is on a separate line, and develop your navigation with the user in mind at all times.

Check and test your site

This is obvious, but is one of the most overlooked areas of site development. It does not take long to check your site for broken links, but time and time

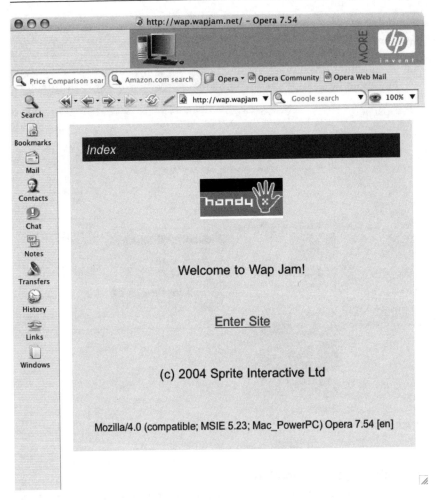

Figure 13.4 *WAPJam in the Opera Browser*

again we see commercial sites that have dead links. This is even more of a turn-off for users in the unfamiliar WAP environment than it is in the web environment, and will present a negative, lazy image of your brand. You also need to test your site on a variety of handsets on a variety of networks. An emulator is not enough; whether for Java applications and games or WAP sites, you should always test it on all the handsets you think will be viewing the site, and on all the networks the site will be available to, as you will undoubtedly find problems. The interaction of a phone, a WAP gateway and a WAP site is not predictable, and testing will save you a lot of grief later on down the line. You can also test your site using the Opera Browser (Figure 13.4), which lets you view sites on your desktop computer; however, this should never be used as an alternative to a real handset.

Easy access

Make it easy for the user to type your site URL – for example, wap.wapjam.net. Too often we have seen a company with a long URL that would be hard enough for a user to type on a computer keyboard, let alone a phone handset. Ideally the URL should be the same as your web URL, which is possible by using a script to detect which type of browser is looking at your site. Alternatively you could use the 'wap' prefix, so www.wapjam.net becomes wap.wapjam.net and so on.

Images

Be careful with image use. Many images will render differently on different handsets, or not even render at all, as some older handsets have size restrictions on the images they can display. Well-used images such as icons and headers can add a lot to the user experience, enhancing a boring text-only site (see Figure 13.5). The trick here is to test what you are developing on a number of different handsets, and be aware of the limitations of the phones you are developing for.

User input

Make sure that the user doesn't have to enter any unnecessary information or fill in long forms. Text input on a handset is hard at the best of times, and you should bear this in mind. Very few phones on the market have any kind of

Figure 13.5 *Good use of images on the Sprite lifestyle WAP page for Orange – reproduced with permission*

keyboard device, and most of the phones you will be developing your site for will have standard input buttons. To get around this offer drop-down menus and lists wherever possible, and when text entry is totally necessary use a search mechanism where the user types in letters and gets a list of options back. Forms should be pre-populated with the most common information in order to save on user input, allowing the user to modify it afterwards.

Communicate

You should always let the user know what is happening. On a WAP site, things take a lot longer than they do on a website. You may have a number of screens for a user to go through to enter information; if so, tell them. If something is going to take a long time to load or download, tell the site users; they may close the connection to the site if they think it has frozen up while something is actually happening in the background. Site users are generally happier if they know what is going on or what is expected of them, so guide them through whatever processes on the site they need to complete – you could, for example, let them know where they are on a step-by-step basis by saying 'step 1 of 3' on the first page of a three-page form.

Logging in

Make sure users don't need to log in or register right up until the point when they have to complete a transaction. This will encourage them to explore your site and give them a reason for entering their details; they will know what is coming. If users have to register or log in before they can even look at your site, then this can be an immediate put-off. If you can, you should allow for auto log-in; this will depend on whether the user's phone is set up to accept cookies, – many new handsets are.

Make sure your site is appropriate

Making sure you have a relevant site that actually works as a WAP site is essential. If your website consists of pages and pages of text, this will not be ideal for a WAP site. Rather than developing a cut-down version of your website, try to see where your WAP site can provide added value. Make sure the content on the site is totally relevant and of use to the phone user; you need to work within the limits of the technology to provide the best possible service.

Wireless Mark-up Language

Wireless Mark-up Language (WML) is a mark-up language designed for displaying content on WAP devices. It is part of the WAP application environment, and is the equivalent of HTML for the web. WML is based on XML, and is derived from xHTML (the XML version of HTML). There are, however, many differences between WML and HTML. One of the main ones is that WML has a different mechanism for linking between pages, which are called 'cards'. WML browsers are a lot less flexible than HTML browsers, and many are currently not tolerant of page errors. WML browsers also enforce the requirement of matching closing tags. The browsers in WAP devices read the WML of a 'card' and interpret it to produce the page that users see on their handset. To get around the limited functionality of WAP devices, such as limited processing power and limited memory, WML uses the 'card' system, with pages organized into 'decks'. Each page or 'card' is the basic unit of navigation and the user interface. A 'deck' is the equivalent of a web page, and a 'card' is a portion of that page that can be seen on the screen at any one time. The user can only view one card at a time, but WML browsers read the whole deck from the server to minimize interaction with the server, which would create lag. Such lag would make your site appear to be slow. When developing for WML you will need to always be aware of the limitations and issues related to screen boundaries when writing code for cards.

Figure 13.6 provides an example of WML code.

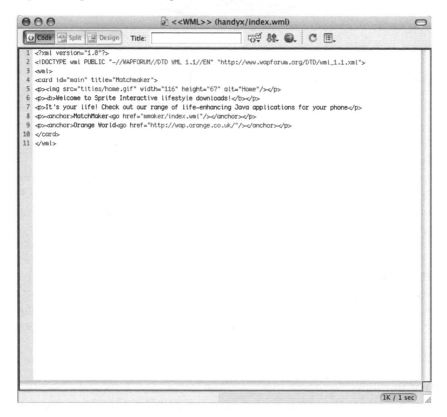

Figure 13.6 *Example WML code*

Figure 13.7 *Phone 'soft keys' – reproduced with permission*

Developer tips

We have put together a number of more technical tips for WAP site developers, to help you best take advantage of the technology.

Soft keys

Keep right and left soft key labels short, as some handsets only display the first few characters. This goes for developing any application that uses the soft keys. It is worth replicating soft keys (Figure 13.7) with a link on the page as well, as on some handsets soft keys are not intuitive.

<go> tags

When linking to a card that has already been visited don't use the <go> tag, as it will re-load the card and extend the history stack, which can cause problems with devices with limited memory. You should use the <prev> and <exit> commands instead to retrieve the page from the history stack.

Dial through

You should use the 'wtai://wp/mc' command to allow users to dial a number directly simply by clicking on the link. This is not supported by all handsets, but makes life much easier for users. You should also think about how you display numbers on pages. Some phones that do not support the above function have the ability to 'capture' numbers written on pages to enable the user to dial them or save them. Be careful not to format numbers with digits (such as brackets), and list each number on a page in as simple a format as possible.

Format attributes

There are problems with format tags, which allow you to constrain the user to a particular set of letters or numbers when filling in a form. On some devices the implementation of this feature is less than friendly, requiring users manually to enter digits such as colons and full stops in the middle of date or time fields, but with no prompt, and refusing to accept the entry until they get it right. For numerical entries you should constrain the entry to numbers or allow for free text entry, and point out in the text on the page how the user should be formatting their entry.

The <prev> action

Make sure you include this on every page of your site, otherwise some handsets will simply not be able to navigate backwards. You should also put it on the first page of your site, otherwise you could trap the user into your site. This may seem like a good idea, but is hardly going to endear you to a potential customer!

Disabling caching

The instructions to disable caching vary for each handset, so you need to be aware of this when developing. If you are presenting timely information (such as up-to-the-minute travel information) that you don't want to be cacheable, then you should think about displaying the time at the top of the page with a brief explanation of the caching system and a 'refresh' link to prompt the user to refresh the page for the latest information.

Deck size

Make sure you don't exceed around 1 kilobyte per deck for optimum performance. This size restriction will change in years to come as faster networks and handsets become more widespread, but currently you will need to provide an optimum service for a wide range of networks and handsets, so sticking to a lower size will get around device limitations.

Style tags and tables

Many of the most popular handsets do not support style tags or tables, so make sure you know the limitations of what you are developing for. Style tags and tables are really not necessary on a WAP site unless you are going to use sophisticated browser detection to ensure that the correct formatting is applied to the correct handset. As more advanced handsets become more widespread, you will be able to integrate style tags and tables into your WAP site.

Top WAP sites

There are many WAP sites out there of varying quality, but we've chosen a few of the best for you to check out as great examples of innovative, well thought-out WAP design:

- mobile.google.com – search and access Google's online information on your mobile
- wap.Samsungmobile.com – Samsung's mobile downloads site, with constantly updated downloads presented in a clear way to the user
- wap.wapjam.net – Sprite's WAP site with simple user interface and navigation allowing users to get to and download content in a friendly, well thought-out manner
- Wap.sonyericsson.com – a slick, stylish WAP site
- www.bbc.co.uk/mobile – information from the BBC
- uk.mobile.yahoo.com – Yahoo! services, including Yahoo!mail and Yahoo! news direct to your phone; this is a great example of a site that has a lot of fresh information
- www.amazon.co.uk/mobile
- pocketdoctor.co.uk – medical information on your handset; the lack of images is made up for by the rich information on offer
- wap.beachwizard.com – surf information on any beach in Europe
- mobile.nationalrail.co.uk – national rail timetables
- Mobileload, at wap.mobileload.com – a great selection of games and entertainment.

The long-term future of WAP

WAP today is still tied to a web-based mindset in many people's minds, which leads them to see it as just a technology – a means, that gives mobiles access to the Internet. However, WAP is much more than just a way to access the Internet, and features many new network protocols that can enable a new and completely different kind of content network than that of the standard Internet. WAP technology today exists in a very primitive form compared to how it will evolve; it defines a workable alternative to the web for content delivery of all sorts, and as handsets grow in power we should see a convergence between web and WAP into a single standard. Owing to the flexibility of WAP it can be easily adapted, and we should see some exciting uses of the technology as it is developed into the future.

Chapter 14

Case studies

Voltimum

The challenge

Voltimum is an electrical contractor's portal launched by some of the major players in the electrical industry – Philips, Pirelli, Osram, Schnieder Electric, Nexans ABB and Legrand. The main feature of Voltimum is the ability for electrical contractors to log on and find out real-time information about electrical products for the design, specification and estimation of electrical projects. The site also contains up-to-date legislation and industry news. Sprite Interactive was commissioned to develop a mobile window to the site. This took the form of a Java application, enabling us to serve up product data to the user's handset in real time. As well as the WAP site, Voltimum wanted to extend their mobile offering with an MMS scanning service.

The solution

The final solution was template-driven – we developed one universal template, product page templates for different product categories and a legislation page template. The products on the site are indexed by brand and product type. For each product category we identified which product data would be most important to the user, to be fed through to the Java application taking into account the space constraints of the mobile phone. Voltimum has provided an xml data feed to Sprite for the products and this updates the list on the phone in real time, enabling Voltimum to add or remove products and update descriptions. Product price data are also updated in the application in real time through an

Figure 14.1 *The Voltimum WAP site*

xml feed, giving electrical contractors immediate access to prices for project specification.

We used MMS technology to develop a barcode scanning application that can read bar codes from photographs as they are sent through to it. The application sits on our server, and when electrical contractors want information about a product all they need to do is take a photo of the bar code using their camera phone, making sure to line the bar code up properly in the viewfinder, and then MMS it to us. The application does the rest, reading the bar code and returning to the contractor information about that product in MMS format or as a deep WAP link to the Voltimum WAP site (Figure 14.1).

TONI&GUY (1)

The challenge
The challenge was to drive more customers to salons on quiet days during the week, using mobile technology.

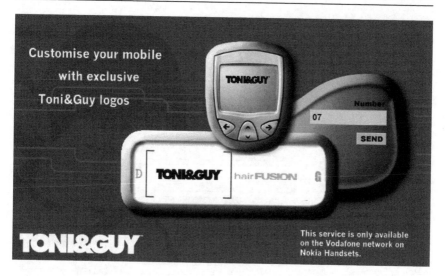

Figure 14.2 *TONI&GUY mobile logo selector*

The solution

Sprite was the first company in the UK to use digital vouchers for TONI&GUY. The digital vouchers took the form of TONI&GUY logos delivered from the TONI&GUY website to a user's handset (Figure 14.2). To redeem the voucher the customer had to take their handset to a participating TONI&GUY salon, and each voucher entitled the customer to a discount on a haircut. The aim of the campaign was to get customers into salons on quiet days, and it was a success across all the participating salons. However, the conversion rate was not as high as expected; of 250 logos downloaded in one area, only 25 people turned up for a haircut. Even so, this was a considerable number for a previously quiet day.

We also plugged in an SMS composer into the TONI&GUY back office system, allowing salons and staff at TONI&GUY to send out mass SMS messages. This system became a powerful communication tool, both internally in the management of the TONI&GUY owned salons and externally, as salons used the technology to reach customers on quiet days offering them discounts if they turned up in the salon with the text message on screen. These initiatives were some of the first of their kind in the UK, and still remain ground-breaking examples of cross-media promotion, receiving coverage in a number of marketing journals, including *Revolution*.

TONI&GUY (2)

The challenge

The challenge was to use mobile technology to distribute the latest TONI&GUY haircuts. TONI&GUY was one of the first fashion brands to embrace mobile

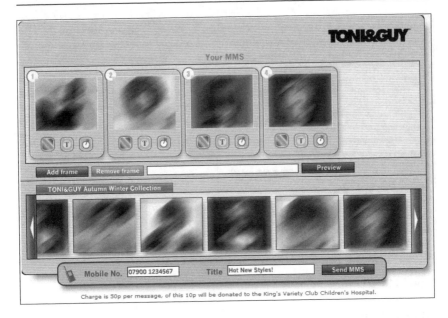

Figure 14.3 *TONI&GUY MMS composer*

technology, and it has always been at the forefront of mobile development. TONI&GUY wanted to further its online strategy by launching an MMS service for its customers.

The solution

Sprite developed the first web-based MMS message composer for TONI&GUY, which allowed users to download haircuts and style collections from the site to their phones (Figure 14.3). This was done through a simple, graphic-rich web-based interface; users simply had to select the collections they wanted delivered to their phone, enter their number and network information, and the MMS was dispatched. Sprite worked with Netsize to develop the billing and delivery infrastructure, and downloads could be tracked in real time, with a web-based back office system. This enabled users of the TONI&GUY site to share potential new styles with their friends and show them to a stylist when visiting a salon.

T-Mobile

The challenge

T-Mobile approached Sprite to build the official UEFA 2004 European Championships Mobile Quiz application and WAP service after seeing the success of our Football Mobile Quiz on their network.

The solution

We worked closely with T-Mobile to define the functionality of the products. There were three elements to the project:

1 *An SMS quiz*. To register for the quiz, the user sent a message to a shortcode. Each day users were sent out three multiple-choice questions, and they then had to respond with what they thought was the correct answer. Fifty randomly chosen winners (people who had answered the most questions correctly) were announced at the end of each week as winning a prize. The correct answers to the questions were published on the WAP site.

2 *Java*. There was a downloadable UEFA European Championships Quiz Java game. This featured 500 multiple-choice questions on the history of the European Championships. When the quiz was complete the user was given a shortcode, and the first ten people from each country to text to the shortcode won a prize.

3 *WAP*. There was also a WAP site with an up-to-the-minute Euro Championships quiz on it. To use this site, a user first needed to register on the site with a unique username. This username allowed the user to rank on the quiz leaderboard. At the end of each week during the Championships, 50 questions were added to the site on the previous week's football. The aim was for the user to log on each week and answer the 50 questions. Old questions were archived for users who registered late, so they could catch up on them. Throughout the Championships the leaderboard showed which user had answered the most questions correctly. At the end of the Championships the user who had answered the most questions correctly won a prize.

It was decided to develop the project in four main languages: English, German, Dutch and Czech. The questions were written in-house and the translations contracted out to a network of external translators. The questions were translated and proof-read in each language, and then compiled in-house. All quality assurance (QA) and testing were carried out in-house, with particular attention paid to the replication of language-specific characters (accents, etc.). The service was launched on T-Mobile to coincide with the UFEA 2004 Championship, and went on to become a huge success on the network (see Figure 14.4).

Orange

The challenge

Sprite is one of the biggest contributors of content to Orange, and because of the volume of content we submit to them Orange approached us to plug our content directly into the Orange World WAP Portal. This has given Sprite

Figure 14.4 *The T-Mobile UEFA 2004 Quiz – reproduced with permission*

a window into Orange World to present content to customers and bill them directly. One of the main issues we faced was how to maintain security of data whilst interfacing directly with a high number of Orange users.

The solution

Orange provided Sprite with a document entitled '3rd Part Guidelines for WAP Content Integration', which was followed closely throughout the design and production stages. To integrate with the Orange system the Web Services Definition Language (WSDL) information was provided by Orange as an XML feed; this provided the description of the available services, the parameters required to call them and the types returned.

Sprite was to take full responsibility for the presentation of all our content on the Orange World portal, so the next part of the design stage was to decide on a consistent look and feel. Throughout the design process device constraints had to be considered carefully, as Orange World can be viewed on a range of handsets all with varying capabilities.

To ensure security, Sprite had to implement a number of security measures recommended by Orange – including IP restrictions, referrer checks, restricting the

Figure 14.5 *The Sprite lifestyle area on Orange – reproduced with permission*

use of bookmarks, and using sessions in order to effectively manage users on the system and negate the possibility of bookmarking content.

Testing was involved because the Orange portal can be accessed by over 100 different WAP phones. Orange provided testing guidelines to help Sprite through the testing procedure, and these were followed closely. The key areas that were tested were links on all the pages – checking that the main path through the site worked and checking that if a customer got things wrong the site still worked. Initial web-based testing of the WAP pages (through the Opera browser) was followed by in-house phone-based testing on a wide range of phones, from black and white through to high-end colour handsets.

Figure 14.5 illustrates the Sprite lifestyle area on Orange.

Netsize

The challenge

Netsize is one of the worldwide leaders for mobile business and entertainment solutions, providing direct network connectivity over a range of channels including SMS, MMS and WAP. Netsize and Sprite were to work in partnership

Figure 14.6 *The Netsize MMS composer*

to develop a web-based MMS composer for O2 (Figure 14.6); this was the first product of its type developed in the UK.

The solution

Sprite worked with Netsize to produce a planning document for O2 identifying the scope of the project, costs and timelines. The main issue identified was integrating into the Netsize messaging platform, and ensuring a quality service. Sprite and Netsize worked with O2 on a profit-share basis for messages sent through the composer.

The first stage of development was to build the back-end integration into the Netsize messaging platform. Netsize provided Sprite with in-depth technical guidelines to describe how to integrate with the Active Gateway API of Netsize to send and receive messages; this document was followed closely when designing the MMS composer back-end. Particular attention was paid to how different phones display MMS messages, and how to use the MMS SMIL code correctly. A password-protected web-based back office area was also designed for real-time tracking of messages sent.

The second stage was to develop the look and feel of the web interface. A modern, chrome look and feel was chosen, to reflect the cutting edge technology used in the project.

RIM

The challenge

The challenge was to produce a suite of business products to be retailed exclusively through the RIM and Handango websites, optimized for the BlackBerry®.

The solution

Sprite developed six Java business products for BlackBerry: My Expense Tracker, My Time Tracker, My Mileage Tracker, My Accounts, My Safe and My Check Book (Figure 14.7). These products were developed to simplify the life of the business BlackBerry user, and are retailed exclusively on the BlackBerry website through Handango in the USA. Each business application has a mobile and web interface with one data source, so if the user updates information on his or her BlackBerry or on the web it is updated across web and mobile. There is consistent functionality across the web and mobile versions of the products, and a password-protected log-in feature on the web ensures security. A database had to be built to hold each user's accounts information in a secure environment, a synchronization engine was developed, and both web- and mobile-based front ends were designed with a clear, consistent look and feel. One of the most popular features of the applications, apart from My Safe, is the e-mail export function, which enables users to send data to their e-mail inbox from their phone as an Excel file; this is also available on the web as a data download function.

Figure 14.7 *My Safe and My Check Book on the BlackBerry®*

Freeserve

The challenge

The challenge was to develop a fully working mobile download site for Freeserve, populated with our content.

The solution

Sprite was commissioned to develop the Freeserve mobile downloads site (Figure 14.8) and to develop Freeserve-specific games and applications to go onto the site, as well as a delivery system to deliver the content to the user's handset. We worked closely with Freeserve to maintain a consistent look and feel with their main website. The main products developed for Freeserve were the donTmiss city guides to the top 45 cities in the world, and a range of mobile pets. The travel guides feature a gallery of top sites in each city, which is fed by real-time data, allowing us to update the images whenever we choose. All the mobile phone content was developed in Java by Sprite, and Sprite also developed an OTA (over the air) delivery and billing system with a web-based back office admin page updated in real time. Netsize was used for a premium SMS billing infrastructure.

Sprite Interactive

The challenge

The challenge was to develop an online scoreboard system to create a virtual community around all our games.

Figure 14.8 *The Freeserve mobile downloads website*

The solution

It was decided that the scoreboard system would contain the following:

- online high score tables, with mobile-to-web score upload
- support for tournaments and leagues
- a database of players
- the ability for users manage their accounts online (secure log-in)
- e-mail/SMS notification of new high scores
- an in-game, real-time high score ticker
- a Hall of Fame feature.

The project had to be developed to work across as many platforms as possible (Java, Palm, PPC and Smartphone), with support for GPRS, GSM, Wi-Fi, Bluetooth, IR, and all other IP-based networks. Scores are sychronized through an xml data feed between the phone and the server, allowing users to see in real time their current high score and ranking position in the application or from web and WAP on their phones. All our current games were updated with the scoreboard system and all future games will contain it.

Figure 14.9 illustrates the Sprite Highscore system.

Figure 14.9 *The Sprite Highscore system – reproduced with permission*

www.handyx.net

The challenge

Sprite was approached to develop a fully working mobile entertainment site, offering games, ring tones, wallpapers and applications, including delivery and tracking mechanisms.

The solution

It was decided to call the website 'handyx', playing on the German term for a mobile phone – a 'handy'. The website (Figure 14.10) was populated with the majority of Sprite's content, and as new content is developed we carry on uploading it to the site, with sections for Business Products, Lifestyle, Travel, Games and Mobile Pets. On top of the Java content we added our range of animated wallpapers into the mix, separated into a number of categories, and used the company AEI to supply the latest chart ring tones. We decided to integrate a shortcode system for product downloads rather than a less streamlined credit card system; with the shortcode-based system the user only has to send one text message to receive the content, rather than go through an involved payment process. The company we chose to provide the billing infrastructure for the shortcodes was Bango, which we have worked with successfully on a number of projects. Each shortcode is associated with a particular product; we developed a delivery system to interrogate the phone sending the message and deliver the correct file to that handset. The site was submitted to all the major search engines, and country-specific pages were built with language-specific META tags. An aggressive link strategy has been pursued to push the site up the major search engine rankings, and paid-for listings have also been used to drive more traffic into the site.

Jamba

The challenge

The challenge was to develop a range of mobile pet characters, using Jamba's cartoon characters, to be sold exclusively on the Jamba portals worldwide.

The solution

Our mobile pets have been some of our most successful Java products; they were first developed for Vodafone in 2001 and have gone on to sell in their thousands. At the time of writing we have a catalogue of over 15 individual pets, and many mobile aggregator companies take the whole range to fill up a category on their website. It was decided to develop mobile pets around Jamba's top two selling

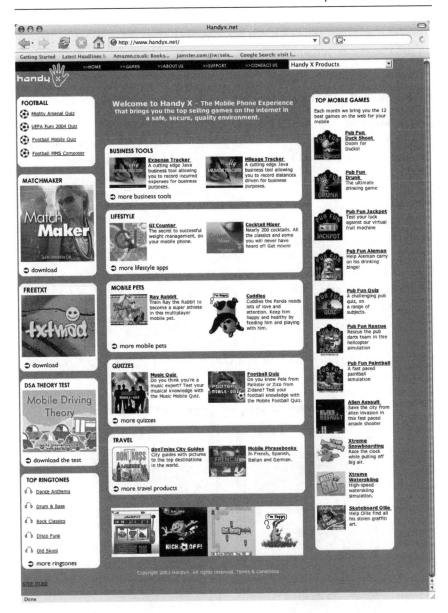

Figure 14.10 *The Handyx website (www.handyx.net)*

ring-tone and videotone characters: Sweety the bird and the Crazy Frog. Working with models supplied by Jamba, the graphics for the pets were rendered and then plugged into our existing pet engine. This is a great example of how we can use content in a white-label style, plugging custom graphics, sound and functionality onto an existing template and creating a unique product in an efficient manner.

These two pets have gone on to sell very well on Jamba, and have been promoted on the web, on tv and in print.

Disney UK/Jetix

The challenge

The challenge was to develop a suite of games to appeal to the core Jetix audience (predominantly boys aged 8–13 years), using Jetix characters and assets.

The solution

Working with Jetix, we decided to develop games around the Power Rangers and Inspector Gadget characters, as well as a generic 'Snowmania' game (snowball fight) because they were being launched around Christmas time. The Power Rangers and Snowmania games were based on games from our existing catalogue, which were customized with new graphics and sound. For Inspector Gadget we decided to develop a mobile pet (Figure 14.11), which was based on a pet from our existing mobile pet catalogue. The products retailed from the Jetix UK website, Orange World and Samsung Fun Club. We worked with Bango to develop an OTA delivery system, using their text trigger service to point to and deliver the content from our server.

Figure 14.11 *The Gadgetini mobile pet and Power Rangers games – reproduced with permission*

Appendix A

Mobile operators around the world

Australia

Overview

With a penetration level above 80% the Australian mobile environment is maturing fast, and with over 16 million mobile subscribers Australia is a strong market to tap into. It is estimated that around 90% of the adult population of Australia now has a mobile phone.

	2004 Millions	Penetration
Mobile subscribers	16.5	83%
Fixed lines	–	–

Breakdown of mobile operators

	Telstra (www.telstra.com)	Optus (www.optus.com)	Vodafone (www.vodafone.com.au)	Hutchison (Orange) (www.hutchison.com.au)
Main shareholders	50.1% government	100% Singtel	100% Vodafone	57.82% Hutchison Whampoo, 12.52% Leanrose, Public
Launch date	1993	1993	1993	2000
2004 Market share (million users)	7.5	5.9	2.7	0.8
2004 Monthly ARPU	45	53	51	–

Average content price (all figures in A$)

	Place in market	Average price
Colour logos	3	4
Black and white logos	3	2
Monophonic ring tones	1	3
Polyphonic ring tones	1	5
Java games	6	5
Quizzes	–	–
Chat services	5	3
Mobile voting	–	0.55 (this is the maximum per premium SMS)
General information services	2	–
Adult content	4	–

Premium SMS/MMS/browsing

	Telstra	Optus	Vodafone
Premium SMS (PSMS)			
Type of PSMS	Premium MO, premium MT	Premium MO, premium MT	Premium MO, premium MT
End-user price inc. VAT (A$)	0.25–6.60	0.25–15.00	0.25–6.60 MO, 0.25–10.00 MT
Number of digits allowed in shortcode	6 or 8	6 or 8	6 or 8

Austria

Overview

Austria is one of the strongest mobile markets in Europe, with a penetration rate of over 90%, and over 7.5 million mobile users.

	2004 Millions	Penetration
Mobile subscribers	7.9	93%
Fixed lines	–	–

Breakdown of mobile operators

	A1 Mobilkom (www.a1.net)	T-Mobile (www.t-mobile.at)	One (www.one.at)
Main shareholders	100% Telekom Austria AG	100% Deutsche Telecom	50.1% E ON, 17.45% Telenor, 17.45% Orange, 15% TDC
Launch date	April 2003	December 2003	December 2003
2004 Market share (million users)	3.3	2.3	1.57
2004 Monthly ARPU (€)	39	–	–

Average content price (all figures in €)

	Average price
Colour logos	1
Black and white logos	0.5
Monophonic ring tones	1
Polyphonic ring tones	2
Java games	5
Quizzes	0.5
Chat services	0.5
Mobile voting	0.5
General information services	–
Adult content	2

Premium SMS/MMS/browsing

	A1 Mobilkom	T-Mobile	One
Premium SMS (PSMS)			
Type of PSMS	Premium MO, premium MT	Premium MO, premium MT	Premium MO, premium MT
End-user price inc. VAT (€)	0.20–10.00	0.30–10.00	0.30–10.00
Number of digits allowed in shortcode	10	10	10
Premium browsing			
Portal	A1.net	T-Zones	One Smile
Launch date	–	–	–
Number of users	–	–	–

Belgium
Overview

Belgium is a growing market with around 8 million mobile phone users, which means a penetration rate of over 80%.

	2004 Millions	Penetration
Mobile subscribers	8.3	83%
Fixed lines	–	–

Breakdown of mobile operators

	Proximus (www.proximus.be)	Mobistar (www.mobistar.be)	Base (www.base.be)
Main shareholders	75% Belgacom, 25% Vodafone	50.6% Orange, 40.75% public	100% KPN Mobile
2004 Market share (million users)	4.2	2.6	1.3
2004 Monthly ARPU (€)	43	39	27

Average content price (all figures in €)

	Average price
Colour logos	1.5
Black and white logos	1.5
Monophonic ring tones	1.75
Polyphonic ring tones	2.40
Java games	5
Quizzes	0.5
Chat services	0.5
Mobile voting	0.5
Adult content	4
Adult chat	1

Premium SMS/MMS/browsing

	Proximus	Mobistar	Base
Premium SMS (PSMS)			
Type of PSMS	Premium MO, premium MT	Premium MO, premium MT	Premium MO, premium MT
End-user price inc. VAT (€)	0.15–4.00	0.15–4.00	0.15–4.00
Number of digits allowed in shortcode	4	4	4
Premium browsing			
Portal	V-Live!	Orange World	i-mode
Launch date	June 2004	July 2004	2002
Number of users	–	–	–

Canada

Overview

Canada is still a growing market, with a penetration rate of around 50% in 2004 and 14 million subscribers. There is still scope, therefore, for a large amount of growth.

	2004 Millions	Penetration
Mobile subscribers	14.6	51%
Fixed lines	–	–

Breakdown of mobile operators

	Proximus (www.proximus.be)	Mobistar (www.mobistar.be)	Base (www.base.be)
Main shareholders	75% Belgacom, 25% Vodafone	50.6% Orange, 40.75% public	100% KPN Mobile
2004 Market share (million users)	4.2	2.6	1.3
2004 Monthly ARPU (€)	43	39	27

Average content price (all figures in €)

	Average price
Colour logos	1.5
Black and white logos	1.5
Monophonic ring tones	1.75
Polyphonic ring tones	2.40
Java games	5
Quizzes	0.5
Chat services	0.5
Mobile voting	0.5
Adult content	4
Adult chat	1

Premium SMS/MMS/browsing

	Proximus	Mobistar	Base
Premium SMS (PSMS)			
Type of PSMS	Premium MO, premium MT	Premium MO, premium MT	Premium MO, premium MT
End-user price inc. VAT (€)	0.15–4.00	0.15–4.00	0.15–4.00
Number of digits allowed in shortcode	4	4	4
Premium browsing			
Portal	V-Live!	Orange World	i-mode
Launch date	June 2004	July 2004	2002

China
Overview

New subscribers signed up at a rate of around 4–5 million a month in 2004. Communication and IT industries are considered very important by the relevant authorities in China, numbers will continue to grow. Breaking into the Chinese market has so far been considered very hard; it is a tough nut to crack, but could prove lucrative if penetrated.

	2004 Millions	Penetration
Mobile subscribers	350	24%

Breakdown of mobile operators

	China Mobile (www.chinamobile.com)	China Unicom (www.chinaunicom.com.cn)
2004 Market share (million users)	207	108
2004 Monthly ARPU (CNY)	100	70

Average content price (all figures in CNY)

	Average price
Colour logos	1
Monophonic ring tones	1
Polyphonic ring tones	2
Java games	8

Czech Republic

Overview

The penetration in the Czech Republic is very high, with most users using prepaid cards. The market it dominated by two main operators. It is the second largest market in Eastern Europe, so is definitely worth considering.

	2004 Millions	Penetration
Mobile subscribers	10	99%
Fixed lines	–	–

Breakdown of mobile operators

	Eurotel Praha (www.eurotel.cz)	T-Mobile (www.t-mobile.cz)	Oskar (www.oskarmobil.cz)
Main shareholders	Cesky Telecom (100%)	CMobil B.V (60.77%), Ceské Radiokomunikace as (39.23%)	Telesystem International Wireless (TIM) (96.3%)
2004 Market share (million users)	4.2	4.1	1.7
2004 Monthly ARPU (Kc)	560	500	560

Average content price (all figures in Kc)

	Average price
Colour logos	60
Black and white logos	30
Monophonic ring tones	31
Polyphonic ring tones	36
Java games	55
Quizzes	10
Chat services	10
Mobile voting	10
Adult content	50
Adult chat	15

Premium SMS/MMS/browsing

	Eurotel Praha	T-Mobile	Oskar
Premium SMS (PSMS)			
Type of PSMS	Premium MO	Premium MO	Premium MO, premium MT
End-user price inc. VAT (€)	Kc3–30	Kc3–30	Kc3–30
Number of digits allowed in shortcode	7	7	7
Premium browsing			
Portal	Eurotel live!	T-Zones	n/a

Denmark

Overview

Denmark has a strong market with a good penetration rate, but it is quite fragmented, with seven operators in total. Most users in Denmark have a contract, with only about 20% on pay as you go.

	2004 Millions	Penetration
Mobile subscribers	14.6	51%
Fixed lines	–	–

Breakdown of mobile operators

	TDC Mobil (www.tdc.dk)	Sonofon (www.sonofon.dk)	Orange (www.orange.dk)	Telia (www.telia.dk)
Main shareholders	TDC (100%)	Telenor (100%)	Orange (53.6%)	TeliaSonera (100%)
2004 Market share (million users)	2.05	1.53	0.75	0.5
2004 Monthly ARPU (DKK)	190	260	250	235

Average content price (all figures in DKK)

	Average price
Colour logos	15
Black and white logos	10
Monophonic ring tones	10
Polyphonic ring tones	15
Java games	30
Quizzes	10
Chat services	3
Mobile voting	5

Premium SMS/MMS/browsing

	TDC Mobil	Sonofon	Orange	Telia
Premium SMS (PSMS)				
Type of PSMS	Premium MT	Premium MT	Premium MT	Premium MT
End-user price inc. VAT (DKK)	0.5–30	0.5–30	0.5–30	0.5–30
Number of digits allowed in shortcode	4	4	4	4
Premium browsing				
Portal	Fly	e–go	Orange world	n/a
Launch date	March 2004	October 2004	2002	n/a

Finland

Overview

With a penetration market nearing 95% the Finnish market is strong overall, and there is fierce rivalry between the operators in Finland. There are four main operators although the market is dominated by TeliaSonera, with just below half the market share.

	2004 Millions	Penetration
Mobile subscribers	5	93%

Breakdown of mobile operators

	Elisa (www.elisa.fi)	TeliaSonera (www.teliasonera.fi)	DNA Finland (www.dnafinland.fi)	Saunalahti (www.saunalahti.fi)
Main shareholders	Elisa Communication (100%)	Swedish state (45.3%), Finnish state (19.1%)	Finnet AB	Auratum international (16.62%)
2004 Market share (million users)	1.5	2.3	0.7	0.3
2004 Monthly ARPU (€)	39	40	41	35

Average content price (all figures in €)

	Average price
Colour logos	3
Black and white logos	1
Monophonic ring tones	1
Polyphonic ring tones	1.5
Java games	6
Quizzes	1
Chat services	0.5
Mobile voting	1

Adult content		1.5
Adult chat		0.5

Premium SMS/MMS/browsing

	Elisa	TeliaSonera	DNA Finland
Premium SMS (PSMS)			
Type of PSMS	Premium MO with one MT, premium MT	Premium MO	Premium MO with one MT, premium MT
End-user price inc. VAT (€)	0.32–20	0.16–20	0.16–20
Number of digits allowed in shortcode	5–6	5–6	5–6
Premium browsing			
Portal	Elisa.net	Sonera Plaza	Oma DNA
Launch date	2000	2000	2003

France

Overview

France is one of the largest mobile markets in Europe, around 40% of the market is prepaid, and it is currently dominated by three operators.

	2004 Millions	Penetration
Mobile subscribers	45	73%
Fixed lines	–	–

Breakdown of mobile operators

	Orange (www.orange.fr)	SFR (www.sfr.fr)	Bouygues Telecom (www.bouyguestelecom.fr)
Main shareholders	France Telecom (100%)	Vivendi Universal (56%), Vodafone (44%)	Bouygues (83%), E.on, BNP Paribas
2004 Market share (million users)	22	16	7
2004 Monthly ARPU (€)	35	37	47

Average content price (all figures in €)

	Average price
Colour logos	2.5
Black and white logos	2.5
Monophonic ring tones	2.5
Polyphonic ring tones	2.5
Java games	5
Quizzes	0.5

Chat services	0.5
Mobile voting	0.5
Adult content	3
Adult chat	0.5

Premium SMS/MMS/browsing

	Orange	SFR	Bouygues telecom
Premium SMS (PSMS)			
Type of PSMS	Premium MO with mandatory MT, premium MT	Premium MO with mandatory MT, premium MT	Premium MO with mandatory MT, premium MT
End-user price inc. VAT (€)	MO 0.00–1.50, MT 0.15–0.50	MO 0.00–1.50	MO 0.00–1.50, MT 0.15–0.50
Number of digits allowed in shortcode	5	5	5
Premium browsing			
Portal	Orange World	V-live!	i-mode
Launch date	November 2003	October 2003	November 2002

Germany

Overview

Germany is currently the largest mobile market in Europe, with over 67 million mobile subscribers. Penetration is very high, and it is certainly a market worth tapping into.

	2004 Millions	Penetration
Mobile subscribers	68	82%
Fixed lines	–	–

Breakdown of mobile operators

	T-Mobile (www. t-mobile.de)	Vodafone (www. vodafone.de)	Eplus (www.eplus.de)	O2 (www.o2online.de)
Main shareholders	German state	Vodafone	77.5% KPN	MmO2
2004 Market share (million users)	35	28	8	4
2004 Monthly ARPU (€)	25	27	26	32

Average content price (all figures in €)

	Average price
Colour logos	2
Black and white logos	1.5
Monophonic ring tones	2
Polyphonic ring tones	2.5
Java games	4

Quizzes	0.5
Chat services	2
Mobile voting	0.5
Adult content	2

Premium SMS/MMS/browsing

	T-Mobile	Vodafone	Eplus	O2
Premium SMS (PSMS)				
Type of PSMS	Premium MO	Premium MO	Premium MO	Premium MO
End-user price inc. VAT (€)	0.29–0.59	0.29–0.59	0.4–4.99	0.29–0.59
Number of digits allowed in shortcode	5	5–6	5–6	5
Premium browsing				
Portal	T–Zone	V–Live!	i–mode	O2 Active
Launch date	2002	2002	2002	2003

Greece

Overview

With a penetration rate of 90%, the Greek market is moving forward at a fast pace. There are four main operators in Greece, and the market is dominated by the big two – Vodafone and Cosmote.

	2004 Millions	Penetration
Mobile subscribers	10	90%
Fixed lines	–	–

Breakdown of mobile operators

	Cosmote (www. cosmote.gr)	Vodafone (www. vodafone.gr)	TIM Hellas (www. tim.com.gr)	Q-Telecom (www. qtelecom.gr)
Main shareholders	58.95% OTE, 9% Telenor B Invest	51.88% Vodafone Group, 10.85% France Telecom	80% TIM International N.V	Privately owned
2004 Market share (million users)	4.2	3.3	2.5	0.5
2004 Monthly ARPU (€)	33	34	27	23

Average content price (all figures in €)

	Average price
Colour logos	2
Black and white logos	2
Monophonic ring tones	2
Polyphonic ring tones	2.50
Java games	5

Premium SMS/MMS/browsing

	Cosmote	Vodafone	TIM Hellas	Q-Telecom
Premium SMS (PSMS)				
Type of PSMS	Premium MO	Premium MO	Premium MO	Premium MO
End-user price inc. VAT (€)	0.25–1.00	0.25–1.00	0.25–1.00	0.25–1.00
Number of digits allowed in shortcode	4	4	4	4
Premium browsing				
Portal	i-mode	V-Live!	–	–
Launch date	2004	2003	–	–

Hungary
Overview
The market in Hungary is growing fast, and it is now the third largest market in Eastern Europe. With colour handset penetration on the up it is worth tapping into, and the market share is reasonably even between the three main operators there.

	2004 Millions	Penetration
Mobile subscribers	8.5	84%
Fixed lines	–	–

Breakdown of mobile operators

	T-Mobile (www.t-mobile.hu)	Pannon GSM (www.pgsru.hu)	Vodafone (www.vodafone.hu)
Main shareholders	Matav	Telenor Mobile Communications	75% Vodafone International, 13% Vodafone Hungary
2004 Market share (million users)	4	3	1.6
2004 Monthly ARPU (thousands HUF)	5	6	6

Average content price (HUF)

	Average price
Colour logos	476
Black and white logos	260
Monophonic ring tones	300
Polyphonic ring tones	500
Java games	1000
Chat services	20

Premium SMS/MMS/browsing

	T-Mobile	Pannon GSM	Vodafone
Premium SMS (PSMS)			
Type of PSMS	Premium MO	Premium MO	Premium MO
End-user price inc. VAT (HUF)	75–999	75–999	75–999
Number of digits allowed in shortcode	5	5	5
Premium browsing			
Portal	T-Zones	Pannon W@P	V-Live!

Ireland

Overview

With a penetration rate of over 90%, the Irish market is a dynamic one. There is a low total number of subscribers compared to many other European countries, but quick take-up of new technology means Ireland is a market to watch.

	2004 Millions	Penetration
Mobile subscribers	3.7	92%
Fixed lines	2.5	60%

Breakdown of mobile operators

	Vodafone (www.vodafone.ie)	O2 (www.o2.ie)	Meteor (www.meteor.ie)
Main shareholders	Vodafone	MmO2	Meteor
2004 Market share (million users)	1.9	1.6	0.25
2004 Monthly ARPU (€)	50	51	44

Average content price (all figures in €)

	Average price
Colour logos	3
Black and white logos	1.5
Monophonic ring tones	3
Polyphonic ring tones	3.5
Java games	4
Quizzes	0.5
Chat services	0.5
Mobile voting	0.5
Adult content	2

Premium SMS/MMS/browsing

	Vodafone	O2	Meteor
Premium SMS (PSMS)			
Type of PSMS	Premium MT and MO	Premium MT and MO	Premium MT and MO

End-user price inc. VAT (€)	0.2–2.0	0.2–2.0	0.2–2.0
Number of digits allowed in shortcode	5	5	5

Premium browsing

Portal	V-Live!	O2 Active	My Meteor
Launch date	2002	2003	2004

Italy

Overview

The Italian market is the second largest in Italy, with 100% of mobile penetration. The high rate of penetration is due largely to the lack of coverage by fixed line networks. There are four main operators in Italy, but the market is dominated by TIM and Vodafone.

	2004 Millions	Penetration
Mobile subscribers	58	100%
Fixed lines	29	50%

Breakdown of mobile operators

	TIM (www.tim.it)	Vodafone (www. vodafone.it)	Wind (www. wind.it)	3 (www.tre.it)
Main shareholders	Telecom Italia	76% Vodafone, 25% Verizon	Enel	88% Hutchison
2004 Market share (million users)	28	20	9	3
2004 Monthly ARPU (€)	32	30	26	32

Average content price (all figures in €)

	Average price
Colour logos	3
Black and white logos	2
Monophonic ring tones	2
Polyphonic ring tones	3.5
Java games	5
Quizzes	0.5
Chat services	0.5
Mobile voting	1
Adult content	2

Premium SMS/MMS/browsing

	TIM	Vodafone	Wind
Premium SMS (PSMS)			
Type of PSMS	Premium MT	Premium MT	Premium MT
End-user price inc. VAT (€)	0.3–5.0	0.16–5.0	0.3–5.0
Number of digits allowed in shortcode	5	7	5
Premium browsing			
Portal	I.tim	V-Live!	i-mode
Launch date	2001	2002	2003

Japan
Overview

Japan is amongst the most technologically advanced countries in wireless services. It also has one of the most advanced broadband services in the world. NTT DoCoMo dominates the market with its i-mode system. Japan was the first country in the world to introduce 3G services in 2001.

	2004 Millions	Penetration
Mobile subscribers	86	67%
Fixed lines	62	50%

Breakdown of mobile operators

	NTT DoCoMo (www. nttdocomo.co.jp)	KDDI (www. kddi.com)	Vodafone (www. vodafone.jp)	Tu-Ka (www. tu-ka.co.jp)
Main shareholders	NTT	KDDI	Vodafone International	Tu-Ka
2004 Market share (million users)	50	17	15	4
2004 Monthly ARPU (JPY)	11	10	7	9

Korea
Overview

Along with Japan, Korea is one of the most advanced mobile markets. A high penetration rate and a love of new technology make Korea a market to watch. There are three main operators in the market, but it is heavily dominated by SK Telecom.

	2004 Millions	Penetration
Mobile subscribers	40	80%
Fixed lines	23	49%

Breakdown of mobile operators

	SK Telecom (www.sktelecom.com)	KTF (www.ktf.com)	LG Telecom (www.lg.co.kr)
Main shareholders	21% SK Corp, 20% City Bank	–	37% LG Corp, 17% BT
2004 Market share (million users)	20	11	7
2004 Monthly ARPU (won)	45	35	40

Average content price (all figures in KRW)

	Average price
Colour logos	600
Polyphonic ring tones	500
Java games	2000

Mexico

Overview

With quite a low penetration rate, Mexico is not an advanced market by any means. It is unique, as there are very few other countries where one operator has such a high market share. Telcel has over 80% of the total. The market is predominantly prepaid.

	2004 Millions	Penetration
Mobile subscribers	37	33%
Fixed lines	17	15%

Breakdown of mobile operators

	Telcel (www.telcel. com.mx)	Telefonica (www.telefonka. com.mx)	Lusacell (www.lusacell. com.mx)	Unefon (www.unefon. com.mx)
Main shareholders	America Movil	Telefónica Móviles		
	Salinas Group	TV Azteca		
2004 Market share (million users)	25	3	1	1
2004 Monthly ARPU (Mex$)	180	225	195	270

Average content price (all figures in Mex$)

	Average price
Colour logos	13
Black and white logos	13

Monophonic ring tones	13
Polyphonic ring tones	13
Java games	35
Chat services	3
Mobile voting	3

Premium SMS/MMS/browsing

	Third-party offer
Premium SMS (PSMS)	
Type of PSMS	Premium MO
End-user price inc. VAT (€)	–
Number of digits allowed in shortcode	5

Netherlands
Overview

The Dutch mobile market is one of the most advanced in Europe, with a penetration rate of around 85%. There are five main operators in The Netherlands, but it is dominated by KPN, which has about 40% of the market. There are also a number of smaller MVNOs that are growing; most of them use the Telfort and Orange networks.

	2004 Millions	Penetration
Mobile subscribers	15.5	85%
Fixed lines	8	48%

Breakdown of mobile operators

	KPN Mobile (www.kpn.nl)	Vodafone (www. vodafone.nl)	T-Mobile (www. t-mobile.nl)	Telfort (www. telfort.nl)	Orange (www. orange.nl)
Main shareholders	85% Royal KPN NV, 15% NTT DoCoMo	Vodafone	T-Mobile	Greenfield Kapital Partners	Orange
2004 Market share (million users)	4	2	1	1.5	1
2004 Monthly ARPU (€)	35	37	35	29	35

Average content price (all figures in €)

	Average price
Colour logos	2
Black and white logos	1.5

Monophonic ring tones	2
Polyphonic ring tones	2
Java games	5
Quizzes	0.75
Chat services	1
Mobile voting	0.75
Adult content	2

Premium SMS/MMS/browsing

	KPN Mobile	Vodafone	T-Mobile	Telfort	Orange
Premium SMS (PSMS)					
Type of PSMS	Premium MO, premium MT	Premium MO, premium MT	Premium MO, premium MT	Premium MO, premium MT	Premium MO, premium MT
End-user price inc. VAT (€)	0.25–2.50	0.25–5.00	0.25–3.00	0.25–1.50	0.25–1.50
Number of digits allowed in shortcode	4	4	4	4	4
Premium browsing					
Portal	i-mode	V-Live!	T-Zones	O2 Wap	Orange World
Launch date	2001	2002	2003	2003	2003

Norway
Overview
Norway is a very progressive market, with handset penetration of over 95%. There are two main operators in the country, and a number of smaller operators whose market share is growing. New technology take-up is also quite fast.

	2004 Millions	Penetration
Mobile subscribers	4.5	97%
Fixed lines	2.3	52%

Breakdown of mobile operators

	Telenor (www.telenor.no)	Netcom (www.netcom.no)
Main shareholders	Telenor ASA	Teliasonera
2004 Market share (million users)	2.5	1.1
2004 Monthly ARPU (NOK)	360	370

Average content price (all figures in NOK)

	Average price
Colour logos	15
Black and white logos	10
Monophonic ring tones	10
Polyphonic ring tones	15
Java games	30
Quizzes	10
Chat services	10
Mobile voting	10
Adult content	20

Premium SMS/MMS/browsing

	Telenof	NetCom
Premium SMS (PSMS)		
Type of PSMS	Premium MT	Premium MT
End-user price inc. VAT (NOK)	0–60	0–60
Number of digits allowed in shortcode	4	4
Premium browsing		
Portal	Wap.telenormobil.no	Wap.Netcom.no
Launch date	2000	2000

Poland

Overview

The largest mobile market in Eastern Europe, Poland has a penetration rate of only 60% so it is set to grow. Prepaid cards are used by around 60% of mobile users, and there are three mobile operators in the market.

	2004 Millions	Penetration
Mobile subscribers	21	60%
Fixed lines	13	38%

Breakdown of mobile operators

	PTC ERA (www.era.pl)	PTK Centertel (www.vodafone.de)	Polkomtel (www.plusgsm.pl)
Main shareholders	51% Elektrim/Vivendi, 49% Deutsche Telecom	66% PSA, 34% France Telecom Mobiles	Vodafone Group, KGHM, PKN ORLEN
2004 Market share (million users)	8.5	6.1	6.3
2004 Monthly ARPU (PLN)	70	75	80

Average content price (all figures in PLN)

	Average price
Colour logos	1.5
Black and white logos	0.75
Monophonic ring tones	0.75
Polyphonic ring tones	1.5
Java games	3
Quizzes	1
Chat services	0.75
Mobile voting	0.5
Adult content	2

Premium SMS/MMS/browsing

	PTC ERA	PTK Centertel	Polkomtel
Premium SMS (PSMS)			
Type of PSMS	Premium MO	Premium MO	Premium MO
End-user price inc. VAT (PLN)	0.5–9.0	0.5–9.0	0.5–9.0
Number of digits allowed in shortcode	5	5	5
Premium browsing			
Portal	ERA OMNIX	Ideas World	Any
Launch date	2002	2004	2005

Portugal

Overview

The Portugese market is predominantly prepaid (around 75%), and has a high penetration of users at about 95%. It is a strong and stable market, with only three operators.

	2004 Millions	Penetration
Mobile subscribers	10	95%
Fixed lines	4.5	45%

Breakdown of mobile operators

	TMN (www.tmn.pt)	Vodafone Telecel (www.vodafone.pt)	Optimus (www.optimus.pt)
Main shareholders	PT	Vodafone	46% Sonaecam, 20% Orange, 25% 093X
2004 Market share (million users)	4.8	3	2
2004 Monthly ARPU (€)	25	30	25

Average content price (all figures in €)

	Average price
Colour logos	2
Black and white logos	1.5
Monophonic ring tones	2
Polyphonic ring tones	2.5
Java games	4
Quizzes	0.5
Chat services	0.5
Mobile voting	0.5

Premium SMS/MMS/browsing

	TMN	Vodafone Telecel	Optimus
Premium SMS (PSMS)			
Type of PSMS	Premium MO	Premium MO, premium MT	Premium MO, premium MT
End-user price inc. VAT (€)	0.2–4.0	0.2–4.0	0.2–4.0
Number of digits allowed in shortcode	4	4	4
Premium browsing			
Portal	Inove	V-Live!	Optimus Zone
Launch date	2003	2002	2003

Russia

Overview

Russia has a huge population and therefore represents a massive potential market. Growth is slow, with handset penetration being concentrated around large cities such as Moscow. However, further growth is expected. There is estimated to be 60 mobile operators in Russia, but the three largest account for around 90% of the total market.

	2004 Millions	Penetration
Mobile subscribers	65	46%
Fixed lines	35	25%

Breakdown of mobile operators

	MTS (www.t-mobile.de)	Vimpelcom (www.vimpelcom.ru)	Megafon (www.megafon.ru)
Main shareholders	25% T-Mobile, 50% JSC Sistema, 23% free float	30% Telenor, 25% Alfa	44% TeleSonera, 25% Alfa

2004 Market share (million users)	22	23	13
2004 Monthly ARPU (US$)	16	13	12

Slovakia
Overview
The market in Slovakia is moving forward at a fast pace. The penetration rate reached 75% in the first half of 2004. There are two operators in Slovakia and the prepaid share of the market is falling, although prepaid still represents around 75% of all users.

	2004 Millions	Penetration
Mobile subscribers	4.3	78%
Fixed lines	1.5	26%

Breakdown of mobile operators

	Orange (www.orange.sk)	Eurotel Bratislava (www.eurotel.sk)
Main shareholders	65% Orange	51% Slovenske Teleko-Munikacie, 49% AT&T Wireless
2004 Market share (million users)	2.5	1.6
2004 Monthly ARPU (SKK)	680	600

Average content price (all figures in SKK)

	Average price
Colour logos	30
Black and white logos	25
Monophonic ring tones	30
Polyphonic ring tones	20
Java games	100

Spain
Overview
The Spanish mobile market is well developed and steady. It has a high penetration rate of around 90% and is dominated by three operators. The number of prepaid users in Spain is decreasing continuously, and currently sits at around 60%.

	2004 Millions	Penetration
Mobile subscribers	39	90%
Fixed lines	18.5	42%

Breakdown of mobile operators

	Telefónica Movistar (www.tme.es)	Vodafone (www.vodafone.es)	Amena (www.amena.com)
Main shareholders	Telefónica	Vodafone Group	Auna
2004 Market share (million users)	21	12	9.5
2004 Monthly ARPU (€)	35	38	32

Average content price (all figures in €)

	Average price
Colour logos	2
Black and white logos	2
Monophonic ring tones	0.8
Polyphonic ring tones	2
Java games	4
Quizzes	1
Chat services	0.8
Mobile voting	0.8
Adult content	2

Premium SMS/MMS/browsing

	Telefónica Movistar	Vodafone	Amena
Premium SMS (PSMS)			
Type of PSMS	Premium MO, toll-free MO with MT premium	Toll-free MO with MT premium	Premium MO, toll-free MO with MT premium
End-user price inc. VAT (€)	0.17–1.04	0.17–1.39	0.17–1.39
Number of digits allowed in shortcode	4	4	4
Premium browsing			
Portal	E-moción	V-Live!	–
Launch date	2002	2002	–

Sweden

Overview

Sweden has one of the highest penetration rates in Europe, standing at 100%. This is because many Swedes use different phones for work and leisure, and young Swedes also have a number of different prepay contracts. There are three main operators in Sweden, with Telia holding the main share.

	2004 Millions	Penetration
Mobile subscribers	9	100%
Fixed lines	6	70%

Breakdown of mobile operators

	Telia (www.telia.se)	Tele2 (www.tele2.se)	Vodafone (www.vodafone.se)
Main shareholders	45% Swedish Government	20% Kin-nevik, 46% Private	Vodafone
2004 Market share (million users)	22	5	3
2004 Monthly ARPU (SEK)	250	175	360

Average content price (all figures in SEK)

	Average price
Colour logos	10
Black and white logos	10
Monophonic ring tones	10
Polyphonic ring tones	15
Java games	50
Quizzes	7
Chat services	7
Mobile voting	7
Adult content	20

Premium SMS/MMS/browsing

	Telia	Tele2	Vodafone
Premium SMS (PSMS)			
Type of PSMS	Premium MO, premium MT	Premium MO, premium MT	Premium MO, premium MT
End-user price inc. VAT (SEK)	2–50	3–50	2–50
Number of digits allowed in shortcode	5	5	5
Premium browsing			
Portal	TeliaGo!	Tele2ComviqGoLive!	VodafoneLive!
Launch date	2003	2003	2002

Switzerland

Overview

With a penetration rate of 87%, the Swiss market is still growing. SwissCom dominates the market, with a share of over 60%, which is more than any other country in Europe. Around 45% of the Swiss user base is prepaid.

	2004 Millions	Penetration
Mobile subscribers	6.8	90%
Fixed lines	5.8	82%

Breakdown of mobile operators

	SwissCom (www.swisscom.ch)	Sunrise (www.sunrise.ch)	Orange (www.orange.ch)
Main shareholders	75% Swisscom Mobile AG	100 TDC Group	90% Orange Communications
2004 Market share (million users)	4	1.4	1.2
2004 Monthly ARPU (CHF)	85	80	100

Average content price (all figures in CHF)

	Average price
Colour logos	4
Black and white logos	1.5
Monophonic ring tones	1.5
Polyphonic ring tones	2
Java games	6
Quizzes	0.5
Chat services	0.5
Mobile voting	0.5
Adult content	1

Premium SMS/MMS/browsing

	Swisscom	Sunrise	Orange
Premium SMS (PSMS)			
Type of PSMS	Premium MT	Toll-free MO with MT premium	Premium MO, premium MT
End-user price inc. VAT (CHF)	0.2–3.0	0.2–3.0	0.2–3.0
Number of digits allowed in shortcode	3–5	3–5	3–5
Premium browsing			
Portal	V-Live!	Sunrise Live	n/a
Launch date	2003	2004	n/a

UK

Overview

The UK penetration rate stands at about 97%, and the market is dominated by the big four – O2, Orange, Vodafone and T-Mobile. Operators 3 and Virgin are gaining ground on these, however. Prepaid phone users represent around 70% of the total market.

	2004 Millions	Penetration
Mobile subscribers	58	97%
Fixed lines	38	62%

Breakdown of mobile operators

	Vodafone (www.vodafone.co.uk)	Orange (www.orange.co.uk)	O2 (www.o2.co.uk)	T-Mobile (www.t-mobile.co.uk)	3 (www.three.co.uk)
Main shareholders	Vodafone	France Telecom	MmO2	Deutsche Telecom	Hutchison Whampoa Group
2004 Market share (million users)	14	14.5	14.5	16	3
2004 Monthly ARPU (£)	25	20	25	15	45

Average content price (all figures in £)

	Average price
Colour logos	3
Black and white logos	1.5
Monophonic ring tones	3
Polyphonic ring tones	3
Java games	5
Quizzes	0.5
Chat services	0.5
Mobile voting	0.5
Adult content	5

Premium SMS/MMS/browsing

	Vodafone	Orange	O2	T-Mobile	3
Premium SMS (PSMS)					
Type of PSMS	Premium MO, premium MT	Premium MO, premium MT	Premium MO, premium MT	Premium MO, premium MT	Premium MO, premium MT
End-user price inc. VAT (£)	0.12–5.00	0.10–5.00	0.10–5.00	0.10–5.00	0.10–5.00
Number of digits allowed in shortcode	5	5	5	5	5
Premium browsing					
Portal	V-Live!	Orange World	O2 Active	T-Zones	3
Launch date	2003	2003	2003	2003	2003

USA

Overview

The USA penetration rate is still fairly low, at around 65%. The market is very fragmented, but the trend recently has been towards consolidation. Verizon dominates the market, and the first MVNO to launch in the USA was Virgin Mobile in the summer of 2002.

	2004 Millions	Penetration
Mobile subscribers	170	61%
Fixed lines	–	–

Breakdown of mobile operators

	Verizon (www. verizon. com)	Cingular (www. cingular. com)	AT&T (www. attwireless. com)	Sprint PCS (www. sprintpcs. com)	Nextel (www. nextel. com)	T-Mobile (www. t-mobile. com)
2004 Market share (million users)	41	25	20	18	16	13
2004 Monthly ARPU ($)	52	55	62	65	72	58

Average content price (all figures in $)

	Average price
Colour logos	2
Black and white logos	2
Monophonic ring tones	2
Polyphonic ring tones	2.5
Java games	5

Appendix B
SMS/MMS abbreviations

A

AFAIC	as far as I'm concerned
AFAIK	as far as I know
AFAYC	as far as you're concerned
AFK	away from keyboard
AKA	also known as
AML	all my love
ANFSCD	and now for something completely different
ASAP	as soon as possible
ASL	age/sex/location
ASLMH	age/sex/location/music/hobbies
ATB	all the best
ATK	at the keyboard
ATM	at the moment
AWOL	absent without leave

B

B4N	bye for now
BAK	back at keyboard
BBFN	bye bye for now
BBL	be back later
BBS	be back soon
BBSL	be back sooner or later
BCNU	be seeing you
BFN	bye for now (alternative)
BKA	better known as
BRB	be right back

BRT	be right there
BTDT	been there, done that
BTW	by the way

C

CID	consider it done
COZ	because
CU	see you (goodbye)
CUL	see you later
CUL8ER	see you later (alternative)
CY	calm yourself

D

DMI	don't mention it
DUCT	did you see that?
DYLM	do you like me?

E

EG	evil grin
EL	evil laugh

F

F2F	face to face
F2T	free to talk?
FAWC	for anyone who cares
FC	fingers crossed
FOAF	friend of a friend
FTASB	faster than a speeding bullet
FTF	face to face
FWIW	for what it's worth
FYI	for your information

G

GA	go ahead
GAL	get a life
GALGAL	give a little, get a little
GBH	great big hug
GG	good game
GGN	gotta go now
GL	good luck
GMTA	great minds think alike
GTG	got to go

H

HIH	hope it helps
HOT4U	hot for you
HUGZ	hugs

I

IAE	in any event
IANAL	I am not a lawyer
IAT	I am tired
ICBW	I could be wrong
IDK	I don't know
IGTP	I get the point
IHNO	I have no opinion
IIR	If I recall
IIRC	If I recall correctly
ILU	I love you
IM	instant message
IM2GUD4U	I am too good for you
IMAO	in my arrogant opinion
IMHO	in my humble opinion
IMO	in my opinion
INPO	in no particular order
IOW	in other words
IRL	in real life
IYKWIM	If you know what I mean

J

JK	just kidding
JM2C	just my 2 cents
JT	just teasing

K

KISS	keep it simple, stupid
KOTC	kiss on the cheek
KOTL	kiss on the lips

L

L8	late
L8R	later
LDR	long-distance relationship

LMAO	Laugh my ass off
LOL	laughing out loud
LTNS	long time no see
LUV	love
LV	love (alternative)

M

MOTOS	member of the opposite sex
MTE	my thoughts exactly
MTFBWY	may the force be with you

N

N/A	not acceptable
NM	never mind
NP	no problem
NRN	no reply necessary
NTK	nice to know

O

OMG	oh my God
ONNA	on no not again
OTOH	on the other hand
OUSU	oh, you shut up

P

PCM	please call me
PDA	public display of affection
PITA	pain in the a_
PM	personal message
POV	point of view
PRW	parents are watching

Q

QL	quit laughing!

R

RGDS	regards
RL	real life
RUOK	are you OK?
RX	regards (regs)

S

SCNR	sorry, could not resist
SED	said enough darling
SF	science fiction
SFETE	smiling from ear to ear
SMAIM	send me an instant message
SME	subject matter expert
SNAFU	situation normal, all f___ed up
SO	significant other (e.g. spouse, boy/girlfriend)
SOHF	sense of humour failure
SSEWBA	someday soon everything will be acronyms
STATS	your sex and age
STFU	shut the flip up
SU	shut up
SWALK	sealed with a loving kiss

T

TAS	taking a shower
TFDS	that's for darn sure
TIA	thanks in advance
TIC	tongue in cheek
TMB	text me back
TPTB	the powers that be
TTFN	ta ta for now
TTYL	talk to you later
TWIMC	to whom it may concern
TY	thank you
TYVM	thank you very much

V

VBG	very big grin
VBS	very big smile
VEG	very evil grin
VSF	very sad face

W

WAD	without a doubt
WB	welcome back
WBS	write back soon
WEG	wicked evil grin
WISP	winning is so pleasurable
WKND	weekend
WNOHGB	where no one has gone before
WRT	with respect to
WT	without thinking

WTG	way to go!
WTH	what the heck
WTTM	without thinking too much
WUD	what you doing?
WUF	where are you from?
WYSIWYG	what you see is what you get
WYWH	wish you were here

X

XOXOX	hugs and kisses

Appendix C
Key legislation/codes

The key legislation/codes of practice in relation to mobile marketing are as follows:

1 *The British Code of Advertising, Sales Promotion and Direct Marketing.* Any advertising needs to comply with the British Code of Advertising, Sales Promotion and Direct Marketing (the 'CAP Code') written by the Committee of Advertising Practice (CAP). This body represents the marketing and media business, and is administered by the Advertising Standards Authority (ASA). If the CAP Code is breached, then there are a number of sanctions that the ASA can impose; these are:

   - refusal by publishers and media owners to carry the advertisement
   - publishing an adjudication against the advert, which can lead to bad publicity
   - withdraw trading privileges and membership of trading bodies
   - refer a persistent offender to the Office of Fair Trading.

   A copy of the CAP Code is available from the ASA website (www.asa.org.uk).

2 *The Direct Marketing Association Code of Practice.* The DMA Code is of mandatory application to members of the Direct Marketing Association (DMA). Consequences of not following the DMA Code consist of settlement of any complaint by the Direct Marketing Authority, which can:

   - seek undertakings
   - issue a public warning
   - terminate DMA membership.

A copy of the DMA Code is available from the DMA website (www.dma.org.uk).

3 *The Direct Marketing Association Draft Code of Practice for SMS Marketing*. This is mandatory to members of the DMA, and following this code is also best practice for non-members. Consequences of failing to follow the code are the same as in point (2), and a copy of the SMS Code is available from the DMA website (www.dma.org.uk).

4 *The Data Protection Act 1998*. This Act regulates the processing of personal data, which is defined to include names, addresses, e-mail addresses and telephone numbers. To breach this Act is seen as a criminal offence in many cases. The Information Commissioner can serve enforcement or information notices to force compliance, and can go as far as to approach the courts for an entry or inspection warrant. Non-compliance can result in fines, compensation and deletion of the data held. The Information Commissioner's website (www.informationcommissioner.gov.uk) contains a wealth of useful information, including guidance on compliance with various aspects of the Data Protection Act 1998.

5 *The Electronic Commerce Regulations 2003*. These regulations implement the Electronic Commerce Directive, which aims to provide a single law across the EU member states. A copy of the regulations is available on the HMSO website (www.hmso.gov.uk). Guidance on the E-Commerce Regulations is on the DTI website (www.dti.gov.uk).

6 *The ICSTIS Code of Practice*. The Independent Committee for the Supervision of Standards of Telephone Information Services (ICSTIS) regulates the content and promotion of all mobile services that are offered at premium rate. ICSTIS works to prevent harm to the consumer by insisting on clear pricing information, honest advertising and appropriate promotions. ICSTIS enforces the ICSTIS Code with the support of the network operators, and it does it by:

- setting standards for the content and promotion of premium rate services
- working with the industry to maintain and update these standards
- monitoring premium rate services to ensure they comply with these standards
- defining which premium rate services can only be provided with ICSTIS's permission
- keeping this definition constantly under review
- investigating complaints related to the promotion of premium rate numbers and their content
- recommending action to achieve compliance with the ICSTIS Code
- managing a system for the payment of compensation claims, and providing a system where claims can be disputed
- publishing reports on its work.

A copy of the ICSTIS Code of Practice is available on the ICSTIS website (www.icstis.org.uk).

7 *The Consumer Protection Regulations 2000.* The Distance Selling Regulations apply to goods and services where a contract is made without face-to-face agreement between the two parties. They do not apply to business to business transactions, financial service transactions, vending machine or auction transactions. The key features of the regulations are that:

- consumers must be instructed clearly about the goods or services before they buy
- consumers must be given written confirmation of the transaction
- consumers are entitled to a cooling-off period of seven working days.

A copy of the Distance Selling Regulations can be found on the HMSO website (www.hmso.gov.uk/).

Appendix D

Mobile acronyms

A

AAA	Authentication, Authorization and Accounting
AAL	ATM Adaptation Layer
ADSL	Asymmetric Digital Subscriber Line
AMPS	Advanced Mobile Phone Service/System
ARPA	Advanced Research Projects Agency
ARPU	Average Revenue Per User
ASIC	Application Specific Integrated Circuit
ATM	Asynchronous Transfer Mode
ATMF	ATM Forum

B

BB	Broadband
BGW	Billing Gateway
B-ISDN	Broadband ISDN
bps	Bits Per Second
BRA	Basic Rate Access (ISDN)
BSC	Base Station Controller
BTS	Base Transceiver Station

C

CAD	Confirmed Advertisements Delivered
CBR	Constant Bit Rate
CCBS	Customer Care Billing System
CDMA	Code Division Multiple Access
CDPD	Cellular Digital Packet Radio

CDR   Call Detail Record
CIDR   Classless InterDomain Routing
CL   Connectionless
CLNP   Connectionless Network Protocol
CMIP   Common Management Information Protocol
CO   Central Office, Connection-Oriented
CPE   Customer Premises Equipment
CPGA   Cost Per Gross Addition
CSC   Circuit Switched Cellular
CSPDN   Circuit Switched Public Data Network

D

DaCS   Data Communications Server
D-AMPS   Digital AMPS
DCS 1800   Digital Cellular System, GSM based on 1800 MHz band
DECT   Digital Enhanced Cordless Telephone
DHCP   Dynamic Host Configuration Protocol
DLC   Digital Loop Carrier
DNS   Domain Name Service
DSL   Digital Subscriber Line
DSP   Digital Signal Processing

E

EDGE   Enhanced data rates for global evolution
EMS   Element Management System
ERMES   European Radio Messaging System
ESN   Electronic Serial Number
ETSI   European Telecommunications Standards Institute

F

FDD   Frequency Duplex Division
FNC   Federal Networking Council (US)
FPA   Fast Paging Acknowlegement
FR   Frame Relay
FTP   File Transfer Protocol

G

GGSN   Gateway GPRS Support Node
GMSC   Gateway MSC
GPRS   General Packet Radio Service
GR   GPRS Register
GSM   Global System for Mobile Communication
GSTN   General Switched Telephone Network

H

HCS	Hierarchical Cell Structures
HDSL	High-speed Digital Subscriber Line
HNO	Host Network Operator
HSCSD	High Speed Circuit Switched Data
HSDPA	High Speed Downlink Packet Access
HTML	HyperText Markup Language
HTTP	HyperText Transfer Protocol

I

IETF	Internet Engineering Task Force
IMS	IP Multimedia Subsystem
IN	Intelligent Network
IP	Internet Protocol
IPv6	IP version 6
IRR	Internal Rate of Return
ISDN	Integrated Services Digital Network
ISO	International Standards Organization
ISP	Internet Service Provider
ISR	Integrated Switch Router
ITU-T	International Telecommunication Union – Telecommunication Standardization Sector

L

LAN	Local Area Network
LAPB	Link Access Protocol Balanced
LBS	Location Based Services
LLC	Link Logic Control

M

MAC	Media Access Control
MBS	Mobile Broadband System
MIPS	Millions of Instructions Per Second
MLP	Multi Link Procedure
MMSC	Multi Media Messaging System
MNO	Mobile Network Operator
MOU	Minutes of Use
MPLS	Multi-Protocol Label Switching
MPOA	Multi-Protocol Over ATM
MS	Mobile Station
MSC	Mobile Switching Centre
MSISDN	MS ISDN number
MSS	Mobile Satellite System
MTSO	Mobile Telephone Switching Office
MVCP	Mobile Virtual Consulting Practice

MVNE	Mobile Virtual Network Enabler
MVNO	Mobile Virtual Network Operator

N

NAM	Number Assignment Module
NAP	Network Access Point
NB	Narrowband
NBMA	Non-Broadcast Multiple Access
NPV	Net Present Value
NSP	Network Service Point, Network Service Provider
NT	Network Termination

O

OLS	Online Service
OSI	Open Systems Interconnection
OSPF	Open Shortcut Path First
OSS	Operations and Maintenance Sub-System

P

PACCH	Packet Associated Control Channel
PAD	Packet Assembler and Disassembler
PAGCH	Packet Access Grant Channel
PBX	Private Branch Exchange
PC	Personal Computer
PCM	Pulse-Code Modulation
PCN	Personal Communications Networks
PCS 1900	Personal Communication System, GSM system on 1900 MHz band
PCU	Packet Control Unit
PDC	Personal Digital Communications
PDN	Packet Data Network
PDP	Pocket Data Protocol
PDTCH	Packet Data Traffic Channel
PDU	Protocol Data Unit
PHS	Personal Handyphone System
PIN	Personal Identification Number
PINT	PSTN/Internet Interworking Group
PLMN	Public Land Mobile Network (e.g. GSM)
PMR	Private Land Mobile Radio
PNNI	Private Network-to-Node Interface
POP	Point Of Presence
POTS	Plain Old Telephone Service
PPCH	Packet Paging Channel
PPP	Point-to-Point Protocol
PPTP	Point to Point Tunnelling Protocol
PRA	Primary Rate Access (ISDN)
PRACH	Packet Random Access Channel

PRMA	Packet Reservation Multiple Access
PSPDN	Packet Switched Public Data Network
PSTN	Public Switched Telephone Network
PVC	Permanent Virtual Circuit

Q

| QAM | Quadrature Amplitude Modulation |
| QoS | Quality of Service |

R

RAN	Remote Access Node
RIP	Routing Information Protocol
RLC	Radio Link Control
RLL	Radio in the Local Loop
RSVP	Resource Reservation Protocol
RX	Reception

S

SAC	Subscriber Acquisition Cost
SAP	Service Access Point
SDH	Synchronous Digital Hierarchy
SDP	Service Delivery Point
SET	Secure Electronic Transaction
SGSN	Serving GPRS Support Node
SIM	Subscriber Identity Module
SLA	Service Level Agreement
SLP	Single Link Protocol
SMC	Service Management Center
SMS	Short Messaging Service
SMSC	Short Messaging Service Center
SMTP	Simple Mail Transfer Protocol
SNMP	Simple Network Management Protocol
SOHO	Small Office, Home Office
SVC	Switched Virtual Circuit

T

TACS	Total Access Communication System
TAP	Telocator Alphanumeric Protocol
TC	Transmission Convergence
TCP	Transmission Control Protocol
TDD	Time Duplex Division
TDMA	Time Division Multiple Access
TDP	Telocator Data Protocol
TMN	Telecommunications Management Network
TX	Transmission

U

UDP	User Datagram Protocol
UMTS	Universal Mobile Telecommunication System
UPT	Universal Personal Telecommunication

V

VC	Virtual Circuit
VLAN	Virtual LAN
VLR	Visitor Location Register
VP	Virtual Path
VPN	Virtual Private Network

W

WAN	Wide Area Network
WAP	Wireless Application Protocol
W-CDMA	Wideband Code Division Multiple Access
WDM	Wavelength Division Multiplexing
WLL	Wireless Local Loop
www	World Wide Web

Index